AI

AN ETHAN WARES SKATEBOARD SERIES
BOOK 2

MARK MAPSTONE

1
MUSGRAVE PARK

It was eleven o'clock when Ethan Wares rolled into Musgrave skate park; a small and heavily graffitied local facility built fifteen years ago, full of precast blocks, banks and quarters, lazily cemented together. Eleven was the hour of beginners. Saturdays were the preference of parents, tourists, and the keen kids getting some practice in before the headcount reached double digits. As Ethan rolled casually around, he felt uncomfortable. Eleven was their hour, their time, not his. A few light tricks would get the legs going, a little ollie over the hip, a manual roll, and a shove-it. Other kids would have stumbled, wobbled, or fallen by now. Other kids would have approached the rail with trepidation, desperately ambitious with their focus, but wobbling with uncertainty as the slide drifted or stuck. Ethan's 50-50, however, did not. It landed with a solid confident clank, scraped consistently to the end, and landed with his dry spinning bearings whispering shhhhhhhhhhhh. He noticed a few lads had stopped skating. It was pointless holding back. They all knew he was there, they all knew he could ride, so there was no point pretending. He popped a frontside shove-it over the hip and ollied over the small spine. The kids sat down. Ethan moved closer to some that were still standing and they moved away. He stuck his nose into his shirt and sniffed his armpits.

Musgrave Park was where he and Ricard Flint chose to meet. Ethan called the time, as it had to be early enough to avoid his old crew. It'd been a few months of careful planning to avoid as many people as possible and it was proving to be easier than he'd hoped.

The top bank had a huge platform which fed into a handrail and hardly anyone bothered with. Most people avoided it and headed straight for the little fun box, but Ethan loved it. He rode down off the bank, floated lazily over the box and turned into a smith grind on the transition.

The coping was drier than he anticipated and it locked up, forcing him to run out and nearly hit a kid chasing after his stray board.

'I'm sorry,' said the kid. Once he'd grabbed it he walked back and said how much he enjoyed the show last week. 'I couldn't watch it properly because my sister kept grabbing the iPad.' The kid kept looking away like he wasn't supposed to be talking to a pro. He said he loved the shows and had watched the whole back catalogue as soon as he discovered it. During a moment where the boy felt at a loss for words, Ethan helped him out.

'You want a signature?'

The kid beamed with joy—he was only young—and Ethan took a sharpie from his pocket and signed his board.

'Can you write it to Matt?' The kid thanked him and grinned all the way back to his mates, stoked. Ethan was stoked too.

It took another twenty-minutes of grinds on the driveway box and little ollies out of the banks until Ricard's silver Honda pulled into the carpark. He popped the boot open, grabbed his board, and breezed into the park looking like a TV advert: light grey tracksuit bottoms, a loose-fitting navy blue shirt, and a beanie. It would have made sense if he was sponsored by GAP, but he actually bought that stuff himself. He might as well have ram-raided Oxfam covered in superglue.

'Hey, E,' Ricard said. 'I haven't been here for a while. Jesus, it's bad.'

'I have no problems.'

'I've seen you blast it,' Ricard said and handed Ethan a plastic A4 file.

Ricard skated off around the park with his

sloppy and lazy style; as if his trucks needed a couple of extra turns. There might as well have been cones on the flat the way he snaked around trying to decide which direction to go. Ethan set the file down on the driveway, opened it, and read the first page: Ubley Psychiatric Hospital.

'Fuck,' Ethan said as Ricard rolled up behind him.

'What's the matter?'

'It's the old Hospital; the worst location.'

'But, I asked you and you said yes.'

His shitty phone connection had let him down again. 'No,' Ethan stressed, 'anything other than the Hospital. We gave you five other locations. Why not any of those?'

'Sorry, I was trying to help you out.' Ricard held up his hands as if he was being mugged.

Ethan muttered quietly to himself and flipped quickly through a few of the pages. Nothing was read. He was thinking about what to do next.

Ricard left it a moment, but his head itched with a thought, 'If you didn't want to skate there, why submit it?'

What were the chances of the location he didn't want coming up? One-in-six it seemed, Ethan couldn't believe it. Whilst whittling down the potentials this was the one Dixel favoured. Sure there was some mystery behind the building since it had been shut down thirty-years earlier, but as a place to skate, it was a wreck compared to the other choices. The reality of pulling off a great edit in a crappy spot slowly dawned on him.

'So, that's it? We can't switch?'

It was futile and pointless asking. 'Yeah, yeah, I know. It's a waste of time.'

'Look,' Ricard said. 'I know you don't get on with my Aunt, but what I don't get is…' Ricard considered his words for a moment, 'Why don't you just quit?'

Ricard's Aunt, and director of entertainment, Celina Flint was fresh mud in the cracks of Ethan's shoes. He'd was fed up of explaining it. Ricard obviously hadn't got the email. His contract came with benefits he needed; break it and he'd lose them: the wage, his bonus would also go, as well as his company shares. And, crucially, there was the non-compete clause that prevented him from having a similar job for any other company for years. They had him by the balls. Leaving was easy; it was the living he had trouble with.

'Look you must be able to do something,' Ethan said. 'Can't you tell her this location is a rating-killer?'

Ricard just shrugged. He had a vested interest in Ethan failing anyway.

A kid rolled up to them and asked Ethan for a signature. He signed the bottom of the board and handed it back to him. The kid didn't go away.

'What's that?' the kid asked, and then after realising it was a location, asked, 'Where is it? Can I see?'

Ethan showed him the label on the folder.

The kids' face lit up, 'When are you going? Can we come and watch? I heard people had died and they left the bodies there.'

It was sad to tell the kid, no, no, and no, to all his questions, but they couldn't risk letting anyone near the building when filming. It was all too easy these days for footage to leak online.

'Too risky,' Ricard said. 'Total secrecy, remember. If anyone finds out, it'll be cancelled.'

'I won't tell anyone,' the kid said turning back to his mates and shouting, 'He's going to the Psycho home!'

2

AN UNCOMFORTABLE PLACE

'You should give it a chance though,' Ricard said, turning over the pages in the file. 'We've found a bunch of photos from the medical archives. I don't think it's a bad place. Look at this double-set in the main hall, and this,' Ricard turned another page, 'There are disability access ramps everywhere and none of them have been ridden.'

Ethan looked at the photos and saw nothing more than gentle slopes and grubby corridors. 'It only hasn't been ridden because no-one wants to.'

'People are just spooked. They've read all that historical stuff and believe it. You don't, do you?'

Ethan had heard the rumours and stories for as long as he'd lived in Ubley. The hospital had housed many crazies; from over-worked and stressed people who needed a break, to the criminally insane. It always seemed like a dangerous idea to shove these people together, but there simply weren't enough other hospitals to send people to. Brand new patients got shipped across the country for a fresh stay as well as seasoned pros moving around long-term to take the pressure off strung-out staff. it doesn't make sense to move people around. Having a well-respected Psychiatric facility on your doorstep brought additional problems. Family and friends moved nearby, and they weren't all happy, healthy, and mentally stable.

It was easy to feel sorry for the short-stay resident because once admitted, it would be easy to get tied up on a course of the suspect medication. A week could become a month, then twelve, easily. Patients could bounce between treatment and behaviour reviews forever, and many were never heard of again, not because of anything sinister, but because the newspapers had nothing to print. People just disappeared. Unless you were unlucky enough to have a relative inside, visitations were unheard of, and the less information being released the bigger the rumours grew. If an accident happened, or a break-out, rumours and panic would spread and freeze all immediate release dates until a review was completed. A true catch-22 spiral of doom, inside and out.

'Dixel's going to explode,' Ethan said flicking through the rest of the file. 'She hates this place more than me.'

'Well, I'm sorry but it's not my fault or my decision.'

Ethan felt set up again.

Ricard carried on with his checklist, 'Everything else is as standard. Three days to film and edit; submission on Thursday and airing on Friday.'

'I've been doing this long enough to know the routine.'

'Look, I'm just getting to grips with this job, and for the record, I'd rather be in your shoes. I'd give anything to skate that place.' Ricard paused and felt the back of his head.

'What?' Ethan was sure he just needed a little prompting to spit it out.

'They've asked me to film an edit too.'

This was classic Flint. He knew she'd pull something like this on him sometime.

'It's not that I'm competing with you,' Ricard said. 'But just that the results are good and they want more of it.'

'N27's ratings are still sliding, are they?'

'Things aren't looking great. They just want to duplicate the success, on any level, so some budget has been allocated for me.'

'Is your location better than this?'

'No, it's a completely different format. We're just hitting the streets and seeing what happens. They're calling the segment, Line-life.'

'Whose idea was that?'

'Well, mine really. I suggested it at the last meeting.'

Ethan was there and didn't hear it mentioned, 'So, there's no planning?' he said waving the file.

'No, just me rolling around with a cameraman. All streamed live.'

Ethan could picture it now: lots of sloppy footage, dropping out with bad connections and nothing much happening. It would be like watching a helmet-cam run in a skatepark: dull, dull, dull. He was sure that it wouldn't go anywhere.

'A few more people are turning up,' Ricard noticed. 'Friends of yours?'

The vehicle stopped but no-one got out and it was hard to see through the windscreen. It could have been Ren, and if it was, Elliott or Chris could be passengers.

'You okay?' Ricard said.

'Yeah, fine.' Ethan kept glancing at the car, and Ricard noticed.

'Hey, speaking of Ren,' Ricard sat down on the driveway. 'I ran into him a couple of days ago and he hasn't been able to find his death lens. He asked me to ask you about it.'

Ethan was still transfixed on the car and didn't turn away to reply, 'I haven't seen Ren for months and no I haven't seen his lens.'

'Oh right,' Ricard had one more message to

Abandoned

deliver. 'It's just that Ren said the last place he saw you…'

'I don't have it,' Ethan stressed and Ricard backed off and took a run on the mini-ramp.

If it was Ren in the car, then he would have spotted him easily. Ricard popped out, and Ethan took a run with caution with none of his signature tricks. When he finished and popped out on the platform he saw a family get out of the car.

'You okay?' asked Ricard. 'Something spooked you?'

'No, I'm good. I just thought I recognised someone.'

'Did you upset someone?'

'Hey? No. Why would you say that?'

'Hey, relax,' Ricard suddenly realised Ethan had the wrong idea, 'I was joking.'

'Oh, right,' Ethan laughed a little. 'Yeah, I knew that. Chill, will you.'

The pair continued skating the ramp for the next ten minutes. Ricard appreciated Ethan's tricks. They were powerful and technical and not expected from a skater with Ethan's build.

'Can I ask you something?' Ricard said. 'If you could go back in time and change anything what would you change?'

Ethan looked puzzled at the question.

'In your skate history, I mean. Like, tricks, decisions, whatever.'

Where to start, Ethan thought for a moment, as a zillion ideas popped into his head, but he didn't let on to Ricard. Eventually, he just shrugged and said, 'I dunno, I probably wouldn't change anything.'

'Really? Well, I would. There's no way I'd want to even live the same life twice. I'd probably change my taste in music.'

'Why?'

'Because it all begins there. Pick your music and you have to pick your crew. Haven't you noticed that skaters group by music; or at least they grow into each other's tastes? Rarely do you find people hanging out who can't tolerate other's tunes.'

'I've never really thought about it.' Ethan set his board down to drop-in.

'Perhaps you've never been aware of it? So yeah, music: flip that switch and life goes on shuffle.'

Then as if the Gods of Irony were listening, Ethan slipped out of a five-o to fakie with too much weight on the front and slid down the ramp on his chest. He turned and saw his board fly across the flat-bottom, roll up the other transition and hit a kid right in the eye rocking his head back as if on a hinge.

There was no scream of pain. Everything went very quiet.

3

ACCIDENT & EMERGENCY

Ricard ran down the ramp to the boy who was covering his face. Just above his eye was a deep, two-centimetre cut, which flapped open, balled up with blood, and started running across his skin.

'Tip your head forward,' Ethan said.

But this only made it dribble around his chin and drip on the floor. With breaths short and fast, the kid waved his hands around as if they needed to grip something and a quiet voice grew into a loud whine like a washing machine on spin dry. Even with Ethan's balled up spare t-shirt pressed onto the wound, it was messy.

'Hold this and look up. You'll be okay. Are you here with anyone?'

The kid shook his head.

'He's going to need stitches,' Ricard said, which panicked the kid further, 'Just a couple.'

The washing machine was now spinning at full speed.

All of a sudden the day was dissolving fast. Ethan had played this emergency child support game before and knew that if the parents weren't easily contactable, he'd be sitting in a waiting room all afternoon.

'What's your name?' Ricard asked. 'Have you got your parent's phone number?'

'Guteck,' the kid said fumbling for his phone and failing to unlock it with a blood-wet finger.

Ethan took it off of him and wiped the screen on his trousers. 'Look, let's get to a hospital and we'll call them on the way.'

During the drive, the kid stayed quiet and rotated the t-shirt occasionally.

A short calm answerphone message was left for Guteck's mum whilst a drop of blood dripped onto the boy's leg.

Ricard wanted to put the heating on as the kid looked cold.

'You'll have a neat scar,' Ethan said. 'The girls will think you're an action man.'

Guteck smiled briefly as if he wanted to laugh, but then gave up and went back to shivering.

The A&E reception had that familiar feel to it; a clinical, subtle scent of bleach, an uneasy blue and green decor, no doubt to offset the backstage blood-show. There was great comfort in knowing no matter how short-staffed, over-worked, and strung-out the NHS might be, the care of a kid covered in blood from an obvious head wound had zero waiting time. A nurse arrived at the side of the boy, took a quick look at the cut, gave him a warm, motherly, word of comfort, then ushered him away to a side room. The same care and concern does not carry over to the accompanying and assumed careless adult.

'I'm not his parent.' Ethan told the nurse loud enough for the couple outside the cubical to hear. 'His parents are on the way.'

The nurse quickly filled out her form, which allowed Ethan to explain how it happened, took his contact details, and those of the boy then got straight to cleaning up the cut.

'I'll go wait outside for his parents; they'll be here any minute.'

The nurse gave him permission with a smile and he stepped out into the reception area, just as a frantic mother sprinted up to the desk. He knew instantly who it was, and slipped out through the entrance behind her, breathing again only once he was sure he wouldn't be called back in. The boy would be okay. They'd meet again at the park in a week or two and laugh about it. Maybe Guteck would appreciate one of those ugly N27 decks the Marketing department kept sending him.

He checked his phone and pinged a text to Dixel about meeting up.

At the side of the hospital building, an old guy was fitting a new parking restrictions sign to the wall. Next to him was a loading bay the width of four ambulances, with a bright yellow metal protective edge. The emergency ramp was a long, smooth, thirty-degree angle, and led up to a gated railing. With the gate open there was a line across the carpark and up the bank for a grind along the ledge. However, at the speed the old guy was working, nothing would be possible for another hour, at least.

A Doctor walked out across the loading bay, noticed Ethan, and altered his path towards him. He was a medium build chap with messy black hair and casually dressed except for a white jacket and stethoscope. He took out a cigarette and offered one to Ethan as his ID badge settled on his chest: Doctor Owens.

'No thanks,' Ethan said. 'Your shoelace is undone.' He almost mentioned that his jacket looked like it had spent a week in a laundry basket. *Maybe he'd been on a long shift?*

The Doctor looked down but didn't move to tie it. The tradesman grunted whilst holding the sign to the wall. It was a grunt which couldn't be ignored.

'You need a hand there?' Ethan offered.

'Just tell me if it's in the middle?' the man said, drill in hand.

'It looks like it.'

The old guy grunted again. 'Well, you can't bloody see it from there. Get behind me and look at it properly.'

After stepping back and checking the angle, it was clear the sign wasn't level after all. Once it was aligned, the old guy drilled his hole and also stepped back.

'See,' he said. 'The middle is never the middle until you hang it and step back.'

Whilst Ethan stood by the curb imagining all the dead bodies of his other assistants in the back of the van, the old guy finished hanging the sign and packed up his tools. The Doctor was still rolling an unlit cigarette around his fingers as the old guy got in the van and drove off.

'Are you here with someone?' The Doctor asked.

'Uh, no, not really,' Ethan went back to eyeing up the loading bay, imagining if he hit it fast enough, maybe he could clear the gated rail as well. It would make a nice photo.

'What are you doing?' said the Doctor.

'Uh, I'm just looking at the rail. It's nice. I skate, so I notice these things.'

The Doctor asked about what Ethan meant by skate, so Ethan stressed he was a skateboarder. The Doctor still rolled the unlit cigarette around his fingers as he looked into the distance. Hopefully, he didn't have any major surgery planned that afternoon. Suddenly the Doctor stepped forward and pulled a loose thread off of Ethan's jacket.

'This isn't yours,' he said inspecting it, 'It's natural. See how it splits when you pull it? It's not yours because you're wearing synthetics.'

Ethan couldn't even see what he held but played along. 'You be careful now,' he said. 'They'll be locking you up in the mental hospital if you keep doing that to people.' He laughed at his slight comment, but the Doctor didn't react.

The Doctor wound up the thread and placed it in his shirt pocket. 'What do you know about the hospital?' he said.

'This morning I knew nothing, until this,' Ethan unzipped his jacket and flashed the file from Ricard. 'Now, I'm an expert.'

'What do you mean?'

'I've got to film a piece there for Network 27. I work for them. All the plans and photos are here.'

The Doctor put his unlit cigarette back in his shirt pocket then immediately took it out again and pointed it, 'What's your name?'

'Ethan. Why?'

The Doctor shifted on his feet and held his gaze, 'You remind me of someone. What's your surname?'

'Wares,' he said slightly uneasy at the question but figured the Doctor/Patient confidentiality still applied in a carpark. 'I've been here a zillion times over the years, so you may have patched me up once or twice.'

By now Ethan was more focused on this odd interaction with an unlit cigarette. 'You need a light for that?'

'Uh, no.' The Doctor pulled his hand back behind his leg. 'I think I can help you.'

'Help me how?'

'I work at the old Hospital.'

'But it's been shut for thirty-years?'

'I meant, I used to work there. I have up-to-date records if you want them?'

Even with rudimentary maths, it was clear that the Doctor looked young for his age. He didn't look like he was in his fifties and even then that would have been young as a Doctor in such a specialist facility.

'I'm good.' He tapped the file in his jacket. 'Everything I need is right here.'

'You know the place is off-limits? It's not a place you should be hanging out.'

'Believe me, it's not my choice: I'll get in, film,

and get out.'

Across the car park, a few men bump-started an old patchy light-grey van back into life. Written in huge citrus orange letters diagonally across the side was a phone number, which dwarfed a strapline: Infinite Security - Professional, Open, Organised, Protection. Call Edwardo Hermanez today.

'I'll be damned. El Gato!' Ethan said, turning back to the Doctor, but by that time he was already disappearing down the carpark.

4
SUB-LEEM-IN-NAL BUSINESS

El Gato turned the ignition and the truck bumped back into life leaving the three pushers behind. With a press of the accelerator the engine revved and slowly chugged up the road until he pulled alongside Ethan.

'Hey,' he said hanging out of the window. 'What you think? You like?' El Gato's thumb indicated the back wall of the truck and his smile prevented Ethan from saying what he really thought.

'It looks bold,' he said. 'I don't think people will miss you.'

'Alright!,' El Gato said then waved at Ethan, 'Come, come, I give you lift somewhere.'

'This,' Ethan hesitated, 'will get me home?'

'Sure. It's done over two-hundred and fifty-thousand miles and it will do much more.'

The passenger seat had piles of parking tickets

on it, which El Gato put on the dashboard with the others. 'These are not even official.'

One ticket had today's date on it.

'It looks official to me.'

'Exactly, that's what they want you to think.' El Gato tapped the side of his temple. 'I'm not stupid, though,' he grinned.

The inside smelt like the slippers from a long dead pipe-smoker. Despite El Gato's window being open a mixture of cigarette smoke, dirty upholstery, and cardboard dust seemed to whip around the dashboard and tickled Ethan's nose. The van bumped out of the carpark, u-turned across the road, and forced other cars to skid to a halt. The gear stick didn't want to get into third no matter how hard he clutch-punched it. When it finally clunked into gear, El Gato thanked Sweet Jesus then touched a cheap plastic crucifix hanging from the mirror, as if a Far Eastern injection moulding factory could have something to do with it.

Ethan waved apologetically at the disgruntled drivers and noticed blood on his sleeve. The more he looked, the more he noticed. 'So, you're working for yourself now?' Ethan asked.

El Gato sat back in his seat and offered a boiled sweet from a bag in his side pocket. 'Yes. You watch Network 27 struggle now I'm not there,' he winked. 'They hired a new guy to manage my shifts and suddenly they needed reports, receipts, and paperwork, and I said, no. Security is not about pieces of paper, it's about Pee, Oh, Oh, Pee.'

'POOP,' Ethan chuckled and looked to El Gato to return the smile.

'Professional, Open, Organised, Protection by Infinite Security'

'IS POOP.'

'So, now I'm in business,' El Gato gave the steering wheel a triumphant drum-roll. 'Going places. What are you doing now?'

'Still the same.'

'Oh, I didn't know that. I thought you were out?'

'Nope. Why?'

'Am-bi-shun! But you still there? Cray-zee. What's it gunna take for you to jump ship? We need to push you a little maybe?' El Gato winked, then laughed. 'No, I'm only kidding. You do good. It's great that someone pays you to play all the time. My old lady, she works all day, then come home, says her shoulders stiff, and her feet hurt and I say, don't go anymore. It's hard out there. I say, you take their money and run, hey? You should know, between you and me, it's only a matter of time before they get you out?' El Gato winked again. It was fast like a gunshot, practised, and perfected, ironically, you could blink and easily miss it.

Ethan smiled back at him; fast, like a gunshot.

'Where am I taking you?'

'My brother's place on Bartlett Hill. He's had some good news and it's time to celebrate.'

'He needs some good fortune.'

We both do, Ethan thought. The door compartments beside Ethan was as big as a bucket and his board fitted in perfectly.

'Hey, don't scratch the paintwork,' El Gato said.

It's not like his board could do anything to devalue the van more than a bad paint-job and huge phone-number on the side.

El Gato continued, 'I sent a picture back home to my wife in Mexico. She's very proud and she'll be even more proud when I start sending some money over.' He drove over a bump in the road and after the suspension settled his head was still bouncing with the thought of making some sweet dollar. He flipped down the sun visor and pulled out a creased photo of him with his arm around a woman in a bikini and sunglasses. 'She's beautiful. Love her to bits.' Two children stood in front of her about eight and twelve-years-old. El Gato had a whisky shot in one hand, a cigar in his mouth, and a smile bigger than his wife's. She had her hand on the shoulder of the older boy to her side and the other on the head of the daughter hugging her thigh. 'We all need a beautiful woman behind us. How is your girl doing?'

'Bat-shit crazy,' Ethan said. 'We're on the verge of breaking up. I'm not man enough, apparently.'

'You should tell her you're getting it on with that hot work colleague of yours. Make her jealous.'

'With Dixel?' Ethan said. 'No way, I could never do that. Besides, I can't lie.'

'Not even a little white one?' El Gato smiled and winked. 'No harm done. You just need to know that she cares so do a simple test. People do it all the time. Better than living with stress and confusion.'

'No, I mean, I really can't lie. I've got an ethical door stopper in the back of my throat. I'll just blurt out the wrong thing and she'll know it.'

As they turned through the streets, the idea sat with him for a while. If El Gato was right and other people told a few white lies, then maybe he could try it? He glanced up at the sun visor photo with El Gato's idyllic wife and kids, then noticed another photo.

'Who's that?'

It was a crowded bar scene with everyone squeezed together to get into the frame. In the middle were El Gato and a red-headed woman in her late-twenties.

'Ahh, that. That is Janette. What the wife don't know won't hurt her,' he grinned.

Janette, Ethan thought and glanced back over at the happy family photo on the boat. Thousands of miles apart and only connected by the man in the middle. Janette's smile was bigger, her grip was tighter, and her eyes were much happier than El

Gato's wife. She was in love. The body language of his wife couldn't be more different. She wasn't touching him at all. She was shielding her children. El Gato gripped her like a cheap Teddy-bear won at a fairground.

'I can't do that,' Ethan said. 'I've had enough secrets and lies in my life from my parents to see what damage it does.'

'Well, it's her loss,' El Gato figured. 'You're a good guy.'

Up ahead a van swerved out of a junction and cut in front of them. He punched the horn and shouted at the driver.

'It's the G4S crew,' he said. 'They have been pretty tetchy since I've been winning a few contracts. They think I'm supposed to sit around waiting for business to come? No way, I go get it. That's a true hunter.'

'Business is going well then?' A broken spring in the seat poked into Ethan's ass and forced him to sit awkwardly.

'Business is not so busy, but everything I do is business. I'm driving you now and what do people see? Business.'

'Advertising.'

'Not even that. It's sub-leem-in-nal business. They don't even know it yet, but it is all going in here.' El Gato tapped his temple.

The van up ahead stalled at the traffic lights

causing him to hit his horn again. Ethan told him the direction to head and sure enough, the other van just happened to be going that way too.

'But I got good plans coming. Super good. You know what? You gunna love this: skateboarders.'

'What about them?'

'Skateboarders like you. I can catch them. You guys are always doing stupid shit, yes? You love it. A little bit of fun, a little chase, and people pay me to keep an eye on you guys. It will be great.'

In Ethan's mind, a mouse jumped on a little wheel and started running, the wheel spun and wound a thread, which pulled a pin, that dropped an arm and lifted a banner. On it, the letters WTF rose up until it reached the top, and triggered a shower of party-popper streamers falling around him, except these were wet and smelt of urine. He ran the sentence again and came up with the same answer.

'You're kidding,' Ethan finally said. 'This is what I do, and my friends do; this is my job. You want to end it?'

'No, no, no,' El Gato spluttered like his van. 'You are being the crazy one now. It is like, we are helping each other.'

Help, Ethan thought. The word kept flipping through the air like a double-headed coin for a bet he was set to lose. 'Oh? How?'

'You know what grows business?' El Gato

accessed some in-depth wisdom whilst staring far down the road, and no matter what the answer might be, *Not you*, was the correct answer. 'Results. I need fast results, for fast business, and everyone wins. You skateboarders skate, I kick you out, I get results, we all win. We win because you are going to be kicked out anyway, right? That's why you are doing it? You know that. It's just a win-win. Fast business. Skate and bye-bye, by me. Yes?'

El Gato was certain that it wasn't a big deal, and even though every inch of Ethan wanted to pop the door and throw himself out under the next bus, maybe El Gato had a point. If they were going to get busted by anyone why not get busted by someone they knew?

'We are still friends though, ok?' El Gato left no room for a response before he said, 'So,' and continued with another brain-fart, 'If you just tell me where you are going skateboarding then I can get there first and *catch you!*'

Catch you, fell out of his mouth with the drama of a Christmas Pantomime. El Gato chuckled to himself as if it was a flawless plan involving him, a rake, and a garden full of money trees. He couldn't even see a hole in the idea and Ethan didn't know where to start with his dissection. It was spoken with the innocence of a child, but with the destructive precision of a laser-guided missile. Ethan peeled his target off his chest and threw it out of the window.

'No problem,' Ethan said. 'I'll definitely give you a call.'

'You tell your friends too, yes?' El Gato dropped the van down a gear and waved at a car behind him to pass. 'We can work together on this. It will be a good partnership, no?'

You're damn right Ethan was going to tell his friends. Every single one of them was going to know about El Gato's new business strategy to go from zero to hero. He was going to be driving all over the city missing his prey like a ping-pong ball at a hairdryer party.

The van up ahead pulled over to one side and El Gato saw an opportunity to slip past. With a sudden jolting gear change and a puff of diesel smoke, he pulled up alongside the van, which then decided to change lanes again and force El Gato into a side road one-way-system. He swore again and took another left through an industrial estate. There was another white van in the rearview. They bounced along over the potholed road and pulled into a car park to do a u-turn, but the van behind them blocked the exit. A shuttered door from one of the units began to open. Out of the darkness of the unit, an engine roared and another van shot out of the unit and rammed the front of El Gato's van. After reversing back a little, as if it was going to ram again, the engine shut off and four men gathered at the front of it.

5

CELEBRATION PAYOUT

'Stay here.' El Gato got out and slammed his door shut. Ethan had no intention of getting out unless there was a good reason. He figured El Gato had already made enough enemies and maybe this was karma coming back to slap him down a peg. He wound down the window a little and heard El Gato try and reason with the men. They just stood fast and listened, almost respectfully, to a desperate man with nothing but his short legs to stand on. One of the other men pulled a golf club out from behind him and walked towards El Gato's truck.

No amount of waving frantic tanned Mexican arms or pulling on the man's shoulders could stop the focused swing of the clubhead. Ethan ducked just before the impact. After an almighty crash and tinkle of glass, he looked up and saw a dinner plate-sized snowflake dent in the windscreen. The man walked back into the business unit whilst El Gato pleaded with the others not to do any more damage. The leader of the men said his piece and they all got back into their vehicles and drove out of the carpark. El Gato climbed back into his van.

'This is the bullshit I've gotta put up with? These guys are crazy. They think they can scare me off like that? I'll show them. Nothing scares off Edwardo Hermanez.' El Gato struggled to get his key back into the ignition.

'Are you okay?'

'Sure,' he said. 'It's these keyholes. They just make them too small.'

After such an incident any normal person would have called the police or perhaps took the time to reflect in silence, however, El Gato just kept gibbering about 'doing business' and 'not being taken seriously'. It didn't feel like it was directed at his attackers, but at his family; his wife, his mother, and father. He sounded like Morse code interrupted by gear changes of radio static; shipwrecked and calling for help.

After being dropped off at Heston's, Ethan grabbed the spare key and let himself in. The music was loud and led him through to the kitchen where his brother had his head in a cupboard.

'You're just in time,' he said holding a bottle of vodka. 'I'm making punch.'

'Celebration time!' Ethan leant his board against the wall.

'Jesus. Who have you murdered?'

Ethan looked himself over. 'I accidentally hit some kid at the park with my board. The short story is: he's got a big cut on his eye and we took him to hospital. Can I grab one of your t-shirts?'

A few minutes later sporting one baggy Jack Daniel's t-shirt, Ethan pulled up a chair at the kitchen table. An open letter from the solicitor caught his eye, which he attempted to read before placing it back down. 'It's all legalese to me. Can you give me the highlights?'

Heston opened a bottle of vodka and began emptying it into the bowl. 'It's good news. They're paying full damages for the car, my treatment, time off, and legal fees, all backdated. Your costs will be covered too.' Heston opened another bottle, 'Then there's the distress,' he grinned. 'I'm traumatised, remember? So, that's a complicated calculation, but it could come to three times my annual salary. Oh, and they'll cover my wages for the next twelve months or until recovery ends, whichever is sooner. The list is endless.'

'Three times?' Ethan tried to do some quick maths, but couldn't figure it out. 'Any idea what the total will be?'

'Two-hundred-thousand roughly.'

Ethan slapped the table and fist-bumped his brother, 'That's incredible.'

'And that's why I'm getting blitzed!'

'Who's coming over?'

'No-one. I need this. At last, I might be able to sleep well tonight. I could have come away with nothing if the Insurance company had dug deep enough. That CCTV footage turned out to be too grainy to identify either of us.'

Ethan picked out a bottle of Sol from the choices, popped the lid off, and raised it in celebration. 'Here's to low-def, cheap, surveillance equipment!'

They both celebrated with a drink.

'You're still getting nightmares?' Ethan asked.

Heston looked at him as if it was a stupid question, 'D'uh. It's on repeat: you dicking around in the car, whacking me over the head with a massive foam finger, the music blasting away, I'm leaning out shouting at the girls on the swimming pool lawn. Just a good day as Ice Cube would say. If I could rewind time, I'd be watching you like a hawk.'

'C'mon, it was no-one's fault,' Ethan defended himself.

'Why can't you just accept it?' Heston threw his head back and swore at the ceiling. 'I looked over and you were almost in the footwell.'

'There was a can under my brake pedal. I couldn't leave it there!'

'You wouldn't have needed the brake if you were looking where you were going.' Heston dipped his mug into the punch again, 'Take responsibility for once.'

'She was parked on a double-yellow!' Ethan couldn't believe he was being roasted. 'If I hadn't dragged you into the driver's seat...'

'I was unconscious!'

'But it was all I could do.'

'You could have left me there. If you hadn't moved me I probably wouldn't be as screwed as I am. One trapped nerve the Doctor said. Just one.'

A reminder wasn't needed. Even if Heston took the brunt of the crash, he wasn't the only one struggling to sleep. Coming away from an accident completely unscathed had its problems: guilt. He too couldn't sleep and replayed the crash over and over, but sympathy and understanding was hard to come by when the only other person you could talk to was in a plaster cast from toe to hip.

A bottle of orange juice was emptied into the punch bowl, stirred and tasted with a scoop of a coffee mug. The resulting coughing fit meant it was perfect. Heston grabbed his crutches and made his way into the living room as Ethan carried the bowl.

Heston settled back in the sofa, swung his crutches to the side, and picked up the remote control. 'Have you seen Wes Kramers' new part?' He queued it up on the TV and waited for the buffering symbol to disappear. 'This dropped yesterday; it took him six months to film; he wrecked himself in the process and it's already on page two of Thrasher.'

'Bullshit.'

'Nope.' Heston finished off a mug of punch and jumped straight in for another. 'Grab a glass and join me.'

'I'm good with this, thanks.' He cupped both hands around the bottle of Sol and let it chill his palms. After a while of watching Wes' part, he noticed he wasn't enjoying it. Despite his brother's commentary, he couldn't stop thinking about the insurance payout. 'Have you heard anything about the mother?'

This broke Heston's concentration and he paused the TV.

'She still hasn't woken.'

Ethan didn't reply. He just focused on his beer and waited for Heston to say something else or the moment to pass. Their silence felt insensitive, but neither of them wanted to know about the mother or child. They just knew the child wasn't injured, however, without its mother, it would be screaming and crying constantly, like the last time Ethan saw it strapped into its car seat.

They watched the TV again for a short while.

'That money though,' Ethan said eventually.

Heston sighed and shook his head. Possibly exhausted with the insensitivity, maybe pitying both their situations and, hopefully, with a sense of forgiveness for his brother. 'You owe me,' Heston said.

'I know, I know,' Ethan sat back and softened his voice. 'This is why I've been paying for as much as I can, but now I'm broke. N27 cut my wage remember? This money has come just at the right time.'

'What do you mean?'

'Well, we're good now, right?'

'We? There's no "we". This is my money. I don't know how long I'm going to be stuck like this or what I'm going to be able to do afterwards. Damn, I still don't know how your brain works. I'll cover your debts to get you back to zero but at least you've got two functioning legs.'

He un-muted the TV again, and despite Ethan's pleas, he just nudged the volume up and drank more punch.

6
THE BAND

And just like that Ethan saw his share of the money evaporate. Getting his debts paid off was something, but there would be no breathing space to have a holiday as he'd hoped. Over the last six months, he'd used all the savings he had, maxed out a couple of credit cards, and gave up about five thousand pounds of his wages to help. The total, at his last count, hit fifteen-thousand.

They didn't talk much after that; Ethan drank another beer, and Heston felt he had enough of the punch and opted for a beer as well. Wes' part was watched and the analysis afterwards helped take the edge off the conversation. Ethan couldn't let it go. He tried to see things from Heston's side, but couldn't. They were family.

Eventually, the day became evening and, after the neighbours thumped on the wall a couple of times to turn the music down, the curtains were closed. The sofa was cosy enough for a night's sleep but it was interrupted by dogs barking at 4 am and the neighbour thumping the wall to get them to shut up. By sunrise, the light cut through a gap in the curtains and sliced him in half. He tried to lie-in but couldn't. The conversation about money churned over and over. He got up and ate some cereal: he still thought about it whilst watching a cat poop in the bushes of the garden, then took a shower and still thought about it some more. By the time a respectable 8 am came around, he'd watched the TV news twice, checked the weather forecast, and it was still bugging him when he unlocked the front door and quietly left.

On the East side of Ubley was money, lots of it, and Ethan had no reason to head in that direction unless he was paid to be there. It felt as if the town's resources were more efficient here. In the ten years since the horseshoe of homes were built, not even a lick of paint had been applied to the shop fronts in the High Street. The pavements were pristine as if the dogs wouldn't shit on them, and front gardens stretched back like forty-foot long doormats. The houses stood like sandcastles surrounded by waves of lush greenery. Conifers stretched high past the roofs to shield the breeze and give welcome shade from the morning sun. Residents here walked around in dressing gowns at three in the afternoon, knew the difference between fresh coffee and instant, and owned box-fresh little dogs so white and so clean. Here, the struggle to decide on where to go on holiday each year was real; Delhi, not again, Morocco was always a safe bet, Cuba looked delightfully retro, Nigeria had an edgy feel to it, which could surprise all at the golf club.

Dixel lived further up on the northern edge of the horseshoe where a small group of self-builds had miraculously achieved planning consent. Here the homes broke away from the traditional and looked designed by International Architects who'd found two million quid in a Tupperware container at the back of a cupboard. Houses had names, not numbers. The Manning home was called: St. Keverne or St. Kevin as Ethan memorised it. Its gate looked old—new-money-old—and swung open on a silent hinge and closed in a considered, soft, click. Even the gravel was clean as if it had been hosed, weeded, and combed. Security cameras gripped the walls and motion sensors hid in the corners like patient spiders. Even the doorbell politely chimed and maybe disturbed a game of chess, interrupted the morning paper, or maybe a call to Shanghai about some financial portfolio.

Whilst waiting, he resisted placing his finger over the spy-hole as he usually would.

A man in his late fifties, mid-height, wispy-grey hair thicker on the sides than the top, stood in the doorway and sucked his finger as if he'd just dipped it in something. He wiped his hand on a towel draped over his shoulder. 'Ah,' he said as if expecting someone around this time of day, 'um,' he said looking back into the house. Finally, still uncertain, he said, 'Yes?'

Ethan grinned wide enough to expose that missing tooth. 'Hello,' he said mimicking a too happy postman on a miserable morning round, 'I'm here to rob the place.' He kept up the grin then waited for Mr Manning to burst into laughter and wave him inside.

However, he did not.

Mr Manning froze, mid-finger-wipe, raised his eyebrows, looked past Ethan, and would have shut the door if it wasn't for Ethan's palm pressed against it. 'Neela!' he shouted leaning his shoulder against the door. 'Call the police.'

Ethan pushed harder. 'Wait, I'm only joking,' he repeated over and over until he let the door slam shut. Through the letterbox, he shouted, 'I'm here for Dixel. I'm a friend; a work-colleague. We work together.'

Mr Manning hit the letterbox with a rolled

newspaper forcing Ethan back, 'Too late, I'm calling the Police now. Leave the property, immediately.'

If there's one thing that wouldn't worry a skateboarder, it's the threat of someone calling the Police. It would take an hour, if that. A Taxi only took ten minutes or for an extra five, you could get a Hawaiian a pizza delivered. The Police were the equivalent to booking a Plumber or arranging a Dentist appointment: you'd have to consult your diary.

'My name's Ethan Wares and I work with Dixel at Network 27.' He couldn't believe she hadn't mentioned it or perhaps she did but hadn't used his name. 'I have ID.' His pass came out from the bottom of his bag with his headphone cable knotted around it. After untangling it, he pushed it through the letterbox. Ten seconds of silence felt like half an hour before the door latch clicked and revealed Mr Manning again. He placed the house-phone receiver back on its base on the wall and returned the ID.

'Not the best way to make yourself welcome,' Mr Manning said gesturing Ethan to come inside. 'I'm sorry for the overreaction. We're still new to the area and getting familiar with the, um…'

'Locals?' Ethan said, then clenched his teeth regretting any attempt to win over Dixel's Dad with humour.

Mr Manning smiled, took the kitchen towel off his shoulder, and walked back towards the kitchen.

'Shall I take my shoes off?' Ethan asked wondering what the state of his socks was.

'No, you're fine, unless they're covered in something.'

The house smelt like a Saturday morning cooking show when they do a close up of a good Roast being ruined by a heap of spices. It made Ethan's nose itch and he hoped he wouldn't have to taste anything. Mr Manning squeezed half a lemon over a plate of leaves and chopped chives until he remembered his guest was waiting.

'Sorry. She's out the back,' he said pointing to a building at the bottom of the garden. 'She won't hear you, so just go straight in.'

Guitar music and pounding drums guided him across the decking and lawn, increasing in volume with every step until he realised what Mr Manning meant. There was no chance she'd hear a bomb go off, let alone a tap on the door. Once inside, a tinnitus-inducing wall of chugging guitars enveloped him into darkness, where, beyond a curtain, a band was practising. A girl with dreadlocks pulled into a ponytail wailed into the microphone, stomped her foot, and slammed her guitar headstock into a cymbal. The bassist wore her guitar below her hips, hunched over it and rocked back and forth with the beat. Dixel sat at the drum kit, head down, arms flailing in all directions. He found a spot to sit on a bean bag then noticed a fourth girl wearing a plaid shirt and skinny jeans standing motionless at a rack of electronic devices. She was the only one who noticed him arrive. As he smiled and raised a friendly hand, the music stopped. She slammed her fingers on some pads and flicked some sliders back and forth whilst using her shoulder to pin a headphone against her head. After two bars of screeching electronics, the other instruments dropped back into the tune and pushed Ethan's lungs against the back of his ribcage. This, stop-start-interplay of analogue and digital, continued for another couple of minutes with no-one noticing the audience except for Digital Girl. When the song ended everyone woke from their focused moment and congratulated each other.

'Who the fuck are you?' Digital Girl said.

The band looked through the dim light of the room to where Ethan sat.

7
DEATH LENS

'Oh, he's with me,' Dixel got up from behind her kit and wiped her face with a towel, then introduced the band: wailing guitar girl was Henri; Anna was on bass, and Digital girl was called Mia.

'Guys: meet Ethan. He's the guy I told you about.'

'Hi,' he said sheepishly whilst wondering what *told you about* meant. It sounded like he'd been discussed with drinks and laughter: the meat-head skater, a lost cause with a screwed up family, who clung on to his hack job which no-one else would employ him for. He was the man who gave Dixel a break, got her into the company, and opened a door which she couldn't push by herself. 'Great sound.' He leant over and picked up an acoustic guitar.

'Do you play?' Henri asked.

'Not really.' He plucked a few strings.

'Then put the damn guitar back,' she took it from him before he could move. 'You have a ring on. It'll scratch the neck.'

'Oh, this?' Ethan said rotating the ring around his digit. 'The engagement is off, so…'

Henri placed the acoustic into a guitar bag as Dixel and Mia packed up their gear and talked about the middle-eight section of a song they were having issues with. Fifteen minutes passed before the girls said their goodbyes and Ethan felt comfortable to join Dixel on the other side of the room, 'That sound was amazing.'

'We're rough at the moment, but we'll be ready to gig in a few months.' She wrapped a long cable around her arm and tied it together. 'So, have you got the new location? Don't keep me in suspense.'

Ethan handed over the file and watched a smile high-five her cheekbones.

'C'mon, it mightn't be as bad as you think. It'll be fun. You'll love it.' She handed the file back to him then walked out to the back room where he heard a hushed and celebratory, *yes*.

A shitty feeling crept over him, and he briefly looked around for something to punch or break until he remembered where he was.

Dixel came out of the backroom with an apple in her mouth and a can of deodorant in her hand. 'I've done my homework on the place.' Her arms were smooth and he watched the particles of scent mist up in the light until the smell of summer sap and pine needles caught his throat and made him cough. 'Too fresh for you?' she smiled.

'It's a bit toilet-y.' He waved Ricard's file in the air to disperse the smell and attract her attention. 'You don't want to see this?'

'That depends.' She pulled a box file off a shelf and opened it up on the table. 'I've done my research. Take a look. There are plans, photos, first-hand accounts of people who have been inside, and some newspaper articles.'

'You didn't have to. N27 pays researchers to do all that.'

'Have to?' she said. 'I wanted to. I told you that place was good.' Dixel flicked through the sheets of paper. 'I found a website with all these old reports and jeez, you've gotta see some of them; the people there were bonkers.'

She went through the list of cases, which made her laugh: the bottle guy - he used to collect plastic medicine bottles and give them names, believing that they were reincarnations of every ancestor in his family tree; another patient suffered from multiple personality disorders and had twelve separate ones, all documented throughout his twenty-seven-years stay at the hospital.

'He died inside,' she said, 'according to his case notes.'

'You found case notes?'

'As I said: I do my homework.' She handed over a wad of photos. These are the most interesting. The inside is a wreck.'

'It's nothing a good brush couldn't handle.' The photos were good. A professional photographer had been inside and made the place look like it should belong in an art gallery. The photography impressed him but the rooms did not. Though most of the site was decrepit, he could see a few lines. One of the benefits of a mental institute was permanent furniture. The last thing any disturbed individual, or threatened staff member, needed was easy access to make-shift weapons of furniture pieces to throw around and hurt themselves. Benches and seats were bolted to the ground, some of them were more like slabs of concrete, the soft furnishings ripped off and used elsewhere by recent visitors. It was hard to tell from the photos if any of them were rideable, but it raised his level of interest.

'And here's the interior plan.'

The enthusiasm in Dixel's voice was infectious. Every picture and headline brought with it a barrage of ideas for camera shots and angles. She emphasised the best bits with wider eyes, and *wait, what about this* before turning to the next page.

The interior layout of multiple small rooms resembled the cells of a prison, and he noticed something odd which made him dig into his file and find the plan supplied by N27. 'Look at this.' He held both plans up to the window and overlaid them.

'They aren't the same.' Dixel pulled the plans from his hands then turned on a lamp for a closer look. 'The internal walls aren't the same.' On the back was a date, but so faded it was barely readable. 'How do we know which is correct?'

'Simple.' Ethan picked his map up off the table. 'Mine is. Yours just came off the Internet, whilst this one came from reputable sources.'

'You're deluded. Do you think someone at N27 did any more extensive research than I did? Don't kid yourself.'

'There's only one way to find out.' Ethan got out his phone and called Heston. He doubted whether he would even pick up as they didn't exactly leave on good terms. The call redirected. Ricard picked up and confirmed their research. N27 had a dedicated team to prove the stories they worked on, as without it the legal department would be inundated with claims.

'We had a good source for those details,' Ricard said. 'A man on the inside.'

'Who?' Ethan asked. 'The place has been shut for so long all the doctors must be nearly dead.'

'Not all of them,' Ricard said with a confidence which irked Ethan. 'We found someone who kept great records and supplied everything we needed. A real buff.'

'Do you know who it was?' Ethan covered the mouthpiece and whispered to Dixel, 'Maybe we can speak with them directly.'

'I don't have the name at hand,' Ricard said. 'But I can find out and get back to you.'

Ethan had heard enough and cut the call. 'Happy now?' he said.

'You're an idiot,' she said. 'From the first day we met, you told me that all these missions go wrong. So, here we are, with evidence that the plans are different and you're still not believing it? Great. Let's go ahead and trust your sources.'

She said *great* like it wasn't great but a stupid assumption only an idiot would make.

Dixel wanted to go get some food and picked up her keys and bag.

'You're not bothered which map?'

'Can you even remember what I do?' she said walking out of the door.

'Urban exploring?'

'That's right. Without a map. I think you need it more than me.'

Back in the house, they settled in the living room where Ethan tried to make himself at home as instructed by Mr Manning. Dixel kicked off her shoes, cleared a coffee table, and slid it across the floor towards the settee. She unplugged a laptop from the side of the room and found her forum posts from yesterday's search results. A few of the posts hadn't been answered but one thread seemed to have kicked off a big discussion.

'It's not what I expected.' She held her finger up to the screen and scanned through the comments. 'No-ones commented with anything useful on the UX groups I'm in, but people have a lot more to say in the general forum where some of my friends hang out.'

Ethan squinted at the screen trying to keep up with her scrolling.

'They say it was a spot for drug addicts and homeless people to crash, but once a new security firm took over, all that ended. There's now a guard permanently on-site.'

'Why bother? What's worth protecting?'

'It says there was some legal action against the local authority because people found storage boxes containing personal items and psychiatric reports. A journalist wrote a piece and things just spiralled. They shut the place down and sealed it.'

'What sort of stuff did they find?'

'They don't know, but,' Dixel pointed out a message, 'this person claims the place is haunted.'

'Jesus,' Ethan said. 'I meant, is there anything serious?'

'Wait. Tracy_093 says the security guard should be locked up, and she'd seen him years ago in another building. She went in with some friends and he threatened them and locked one of her friends in a room. He cut the power, separated them ...'

Then Dixel paused and read on to herself.

'And?'

'They're saying he drugged them and left them outside. They tried to get him arrested, but nothing happened. The police didn't even respond. They were too busy dealing with the fire.'

'What fire?'

'Like, *the Fire*. There's only been one fire around here which could take out an entire police force. I don't mean some old pallets on an allotment.'

'Oh, right. That,' he said. The biggest fire in history happened five years ago and almost destroyed the entire town. Thousands of people were housed in a football stadium for months. Ethan was touring around with his teammates at the time and got caught up in it in a way which made him shudder inside. 'Do they say anything about the sedated part? Like how, with an injection?'

'I don't know. Another one here says he had a bad experience with the guard too. He went in after replying to an advert for photo tours. The guard was nice at first, led him around the building showing off all the details and 'secret areas' then became irritated when he wanted to leave. After that, the guard left him on the second floor in the dark and locked the gate to the stairs. The guy only got out by crawling through a ventilation shaft.'

'Is this recent?'

'All in the last couple of months.'

Dixel scanned the remaining posts for any more details but found people just chiming in with other vague experiences which amounted to very little. She eventually sat back into the sofa and took a bite out of a sandwich her dad had brought in.

'Are you put off?' she asked.

Nope,' he said. 'It sound's like a load of BS to me. Besides, who are these people? A bunch of geeks, musos and students.'

'Hey, I'm a muso.'

'Wait, what was that bit about them being left outside?'

'Just dumped outside. Some people have found themselves outside the building with no idea how they got there. People think it's the ghosts.'

'Riiiight,' Ethan rolled his eyes and pulled out his floor plan. 'Look can we get back to the serious stuff? Is there a way in, and, assuming there is, where is worth filming?'

They laid out the map and identified the entrances and exits, noting there were only a few options. The official routes were gated, fenced, and in some cases bricked up completely. According to other photographers, the perimeter walls were still very solid: no holes, no collapses, and no weak sections.

'If these plans are to scale,' Dixel wondered, 'those walls are six-feet thick in places. Are you sure this place wasn't a military bunker?' They matched up the floor plan with the interior photography they found and placed them on the floor. 'We need Google Maps for the interior,' she said. 'Everything leads into and out of this area.' Dixel pointed out a huge space in the middle of the map. The rest was a maze of corridors, offices, and rooms only big enough for a single bed and a bucket.

There was a smaller space towards the back of the large room, 'This is probably the stairwell.' Ethan pulled out another sheet of paper from the folder for the second and third floor. 'This place is massive. I hadn't realised.'

'So what are we bringing inside?' Dixel said. 'I'm going in light with my old VX2100 and just one LED lamp. After what happened last time, I don't want to carry anything valuable.'

Ethan had a puzzled looked on his face.

'Don't worry,' she said. 'The kit might be old, but it's still good. Leave the filming to me—you worry about skating.'

'Which reminds me,' Ethan reached into his bag. 'I've got a present for you.' He pulled out a small, but heavy object wrapped in a t-shirt.

'An eight-millimetre lens?' She took it and studied the glass. 'This is pristine!'

'It's a Death lens,' Ethan said. 'You can have it. It was mine, but I don't have a camera anymore.'

'A what?'

'It's a called a Death lens because it makes gaps and heights look huge: do-or-die big.'

'Oh, a fisheye. Cool. I've not used one of these before. Aren't they really expensive?'

'Well, I didn't buy it as such,' he said. 'It's on permanent loan from someone who owes me.'

That someone was Ren, and he owed Ethan money. Once he realised the cash was as good as gone, he'd focused on Ren's assets instead. They'd got wasted. Ren being a lightweight in the alcohol department was destroyed before Ethan even got wobbly. They had both stumbled back to Ren's place in the early hours and Ethan *borrowed* the lens intending to sell it. Technically it wasn't theft, he'd told himself; technically he didn't break-in, and technically possession is nine-tenths of the law, so he'd heard somewhere. Besides, fancy cameras are one thing, but good glass is another and Dixel wouldn't be able to shoot the edits he needed without one.

8

BRICK DUST

As Dixel scrolled through more web pages about the Mental Hospital, Ethan's mind wandered. He wasn't bored but distracted. Maybe it was the art on the walls, family portraits by the TV, objects on the shelf from trips abroad, and the smell of cooking from the kitchen. He realised it was something else. Every time he tried to concentrate on what Dixel said, something flashed into his mind: Ricard at the skatepark telling him about his edit for N27. Ricard was a joke and about to ruin the reputation Ethan had created. He wondered, briefly, if he cared about N27, then shook it off.

He connected his phone to Dixel's WiFi and found some recent footage. 'Give me your opinion. What do you think of his riding?'

Dixel took hold of the phone and concentrated on the rider carving around, popping and switching his stance out of manual rolls and wallies. He squatted a little on the board and held his hands out like he was gliding a plane into land, making minor adjustments with his palms. After half a minute of screen time, she was still transfixed.

'It's an embarrassment,' Ethan tutted and sucked air through his teeth at a boneless off a low wall.

Dixel kept watching, 'He's cute.'

She had no idea. Ricard lacked any real talent and his style was just lame posturing. Ethan tried to take the screen back but Dixel pulled it closer.

'Hey, I'm still watching,' she said then, 'I think he's good.'

'You don't even know what you're looking at.'

'He hasn't fallen off once yet.'

'But he's not doing anything. He's an embarrassment.'

'If he's so bad,' she said, 'then why's he been given a spot on the schedule?'

'Because he's Flint's special soldier, isn't he?'

She tossed the phone onto his lap, 'Why can't you be happy for him? Surely the more skateboarding on TV the better?'

Like, duh, Ethan thought, *but not like that!*

Mr Manning appeared at his side and asked if he was staying for lunch. But those spices just made him want to jam ear-buds into his nostrils.

'I've got to go,' he said.

Abandoned

'Already? We're just getting going.'

'We've got all we need and anything else we can figure out once we get there.' Ethan stood to leave but didn't know which of the three living room doors was the way out. A sudden surge of anxiety prickled under his skin and only eased once Mr Manning gestured towards the correct door. As he stepped out of the house onto their garden path, he immediately felt better and reminded Dixel not to forget the lens tomorrow.

'I won't. Thanks.'

He wondered if Dixel would hang around in the doorway watching him leave. He wanted to look back and check but didn't until he reached the end of the driveway. The door was already shut and she wasn't looking through the blinds either. The garden gate swung open smoothly and began to gently close on its precision weighted hinge. That slow movement inched the gate back towards the lock just a few well-oiled degrees at a time. Ethan waited a moment for it to close. He waited, and waited, and looked back at the house for just a twitch of the blinds. The gate still hadn't closed. The blinds didn't move. He yanked the gate shut with a slam.

By nine-thirty the following morning, after another crap night's sleep on Heston's sofa, he was on the bus to the Psychiatric Hospital. The engine rumble sent him off to sleep before it had reached the end of the road. Dixel kicked his leg and he stirred. Moments later she kicked him again. She said the first time was because he was snoring and the second kick was just for fun. Once the bus had dropped them off at the Hospital and rumbled off into the fog they stood facing a three-metre high stone wall.

'Well, this is intimidating.' Ethan looked around into the bleak whiteness.

'This fog is cool though,' Dixel said. 'It'll add some atmospherics to the filming.'

'Pretty footage isn't going to help us if I can't see what I'm doing,'

'Your brain-fog will cause you bigger problems. Think you'll be awake by then?'

'Wide awake.' Ethan cracked open a can of Coke for a quick sugar-caffeine hit and walked up the pavement. 'This way,' he said.

'Who says?'

'My instinct.'

They walked the perimeter wall to the main entrance which had a decrepit sentry box that would not look out of place in a World War II film. The shiny-new brass padlocks on the gates stood out like a dent in a Ferrari. A sign screwed over the top of the old one read: Infinite Security.

El Gato.

'I know the guy who runs that company,' Ethan said. 'This means things could either go well today or suck times ten. He gave me a lift a couple of days ago to my brother's place and told me catching skateboarders was his new business strategy.'

'And how do you know him?' Dixel asked.

'He was a guard at N27 before they started culling contracts.'

Dixel stopped by a row of storm drains and watched a fast stream of water pass quickly beneath them.

'Do you think you could lift one of these?'

'Get out of it,' he said. 'I might look like a sewer-rat but these are actually my good clothes.'

Then she spotted a small square hole in the wall. The bars were rusted thin in places and one was almost eaten away completely.

'What about this?' she crouched down to examine the gap. 'If we broke away one of these bars, I think I could squeeze through.'

Ethan sat on the damp grass and kicked a few times at the top bar until it snapped free of its join. 'That was easy,' he said. 'One down, one to go.' He kicked out the other bar and stood on it to push it flat.

Dixel crawled through to the other side. 'It's okay,' she said brushing the brick dust from her coat. 'Pass the bags through to me.'

With their gear on the other side, Ethan began

to crawl through, however, being larger than Dixel by a good few stones, the bars snagged on his belt and pockets. At one point he thought he would go back but quickly realised going back would be harder than going through. He refused Dixel's helping hand; the hole scraped his shoulders, waist and thighs, inch by inch, until eventually, upon reaching the other side and using only his elbows, he managed to pull the rest of himself through.

'Damn, that was tight,' he said covered in brick dust.

'I guess we're not going back out that way.' She handed him his bag.

From inside the huge wall wasn't a barrier but a container wrapped around them, and the fog, though less dense than outside, still made everything look like a faded postcard. The courtyard was much smaller than he'd expected and had goal posts painted on the walls. They walked towards the main building; a big old crumbling construction with exposed balconies and bay windows on the first and second floors, and many roof peaks from additional buildings. It was easy to imagine patients leaning out over the balconies watching the games being played beneath; the grass mowed and well kept by the residents on garden duty; the vegetable patches; the benches lining the walls.

'I was expecting something resembling an East

European industrial estate,' Dixel said, 'but this looks like it would have been quite a nice place.'

'Twenty-years ago maybe. Hey, are these shackles?' Ethan picked up a rusted steel cuff chained to the wall.

Every window on the ground floor had been smashed, a kitchen had its units destroyed and had more young-offender tags sprayed on the walls than a signing-in book at a pupil reform unit. The next wreck looked like an office and another space looked empty except for a few plastic chairs scattered about. They reached a heavy door with a broken hinge and dragged it open, scraping the floor with an ear-piercing screech. Soft seats lined the damp walls, and a finger wipe over the counter cut a vibrant blue line through the dust. The dates in the visitors' book stopped at 1997.

Dixel pushed out through a heavy door which swung back and slammed into its lock. She immediately rushed back and pulled on the handle. The lock clicked again and the door opened.

The panic and then relief on her face made Ethan laugh. 'Your face was a treat.' He flicked the catch on and off. 'These things were built to last.'

The next-door opened and shut again easily, too. 'They must all be like this,' she said. 'Come on, let's see what we can find.'

'Shouldn't we mark our route or something?'

'Like Hansel and Gretel dropping breadcrumbs?' Dixel laughed. 'You've got your map, haven't you?'

The map, of course. Ethan pulled it out of his pocket and located the main entrance, the reception room, and the corridor to the right of him. 'I know where we are,' he said.

'Oh, pul-lease,' she said. 'Don't tell me you're going to be holding that in front of your nose the entire time. This place isn't going to swallow you up. Let's go. You're supposed to be looking for something to ride.'

They headed into the building through a corridor flanked with small rooms. Dixel checked the right side and Ethan checked the left. They needed something useful, interesting, skate-able, and photogenic. Many of the rooms they passed looked like prison cells. It was easy to imagine patients strapped to the bed frames, sedated, or hammering on the doors for attention. Scratches on the walls looked like they could have been made by fingernails. At the end of the corridor, Dixel looked back and held her fingers up to her eyes to frame the view.

'People really do that?' Ethan asked. 'I thought that was only in films.'

'This would make a good shot. Can you find a broom and sweep it?'

It might make a good shot in her eyes, but there was nothing for him to ride at all.

'Hey, look at this,' he said walking into another room.

Rows of metal filing cabinets lined the walls, six drawers high from the floor to ceiling, all labelled alphabetically and each one locked. The keyholes were tiny clean brass barrels as if someone had recently wiped them.

'You think anything is still inside them?' Ethan tugged on one of the drawer handles.

'It doesn't look like it.' Dixel noticed one of the cabinets—the W's—were unlocked. Its door swung open freely but inside it was empty. 'It's probably been raided.'

Suddenly, a loud, high-pitched scrape of the outside gates echoed around the courtyard walls and bounced in through the windows. Dixel went to the window and saw the security guard walk out across the yard. 'He's leaving,' she whispered.

9

BANK TO LEDGE

They watched the guard close the gate behind him and trudge off on his rounds.

'At least we know he'll be gone for a while,' Dixel said. 'How long do you think we have?'

'No idea,' Ethan said. 'But the place is massive, so if he's doing a loop, maybe thirty or forty minutes?'

The guard forced them to change their strategy. Instead of leisurely walking the halls and pausing in each room, they quickly covered the entire ground floor. Normally Ethan would just hit up the first decent spot he found, but this time Dixel insisted they scout first and choose later.

'The best spots,' she said, 'are never where you expect them.'

The spots she meant were Urban Exploration ones, he'd be the judge of whether something was skate-able or not. The interior of the building was as much of a wreck as the outside, and they often had to kick through piles of debris just to get through the corridors. Anything timber-based had been ripped from its fittings and used as firewood; anything secure had been hammered to death in an attempt to see what was inside; anything soft was rank, either mouldy-damp or burnt out. An entire sofa looked completely out of place and couldn't have been part of the original hospital. The damn thing still had velour on the arms. Someone must have brought it in from outside to make their stay more comfortable.

'I wouldn't sit on that if I were you.' Dixel brushed past Ethan to look out through one of the windows.

He paused mid-sit, 'Why not?'

She kicked some of the charred table legs out of her way. 'Look at this place. It's perfect for smack-heads. There are needles everywhere.'

The room they'd ended up in appeared to be a community room. Old magazines were scattered around, a noticeboard dangled from a broken fitting and an old sofa had been dragged in front of a fireplace. The window ledge was a heavy-set slab of concrete, wider than the others, and jutted out from the wall by a few inches. A rip in the thread-bare carpet showed a herringbone tiled floor. Ethan grabbed a piece of plywood and scraped away stones, cans, wet papers, and food packets. He then pulled the carpet up to make a clear path to the window. The tiles beneath it didn't even need a brush: they looked as good as the day they were laid.

Dixel noticed he had seen something and started unpacking her camera. 'If you're going to do something there, I can set the camera up behind these serving hatches: they'll frame the shot perfectly.'

'Got it.' He couldn't believe his luck at getting some footage so early.

A little kicker was created out of a table frame and a sheet of metal from one of the kitchens. The plywood he'd found worked perfectly as the surface, and fit neatly from the edge to the floor.

'Are you ready to go?' Dixel shouted from the other room.

'I haven't even tested it yet!'

'Ok,' she said. 'I need to set the white balance first, anyway.'

Ethan skated down through the corridor, carved around to the kicker, and scooped a backside ollie up to an indy nose pick on the ledge, then yanked it back in. As he rode out through to Dixel's room, he asked, 'Did you get that?'

'No!' she snapped back at him. 'Give me a chance to get ready.'

Ethan hit the kicker again and repeated the

same move, but a frontside nose-pick this time. With his next attempt, he landed a frontside tail-stall and hopped it in down the ramp; his next run landed backside-to-tail and kicked a big-spin on his way out to land fakie back down the kicker. For an early find, it was a pretty good spot to warm up. Whenever he looked up at Dixel, she seemed to be messing around with her camera angles so he didn't bother to ask whether she was ready. He kept on hitting the kicker and sticking whatever he could on the ledge. Each move landed with accuracy and not much of a challenge. It was so much fun and reminded him of being a kid, playing in the driveway with Heston on their boards. They'd learn grabs out of fly-offs made from a sheet of ply, pretending they were at some amazing skatepark, sessioning for hours until dark. Kids on bikes would try to blag some go's but were fought off with half-bricks thrown at their spokes.

Those days were the best; long summers, and nothing to do but ride. When things were bad at home, like when his board got pawned for a few quid to 'pay bills' or he was grounded for thieving—not because he did it, but because he was stupid enough to get caught, his mum would say—he could rely on those memories to get him through the boredom.

Through the serving hatch in the wall, Ethan saw Dixel's VX2100 on what appeared to be a very flimsy tripod. One whack of the legs and it would surely buckle. She was elsewhere, but at least she hadn't put the fisheye on yet. He wanted to ask if she was okay but had already noticed a touch of Viking-temperament in her attitude towards him. She'd shout when she was ready, he was sure of it. Besides, now his legs were warmed up, he knew he could start stepping it up a gear. A front-flip to five-o stall, holding it for a moment then hopping in back-side to fakie; next, and going frontside again, he caught a kickflip-to-tail. Another glance back at Dixel: this time she'd moved the camera between a doorway and was adjusting the tripod height.

Filming was a faff he decided. All gear and no-idea was the mantra he tutted to himself, whenever he ran into kids with cameras these days. They seemed to want to shoot like a tourist, instead of getting low and rolling with the skater. Distance filming was perfect for wildlife photography but a camera needed to move, to vibrate, and catch the pebbles and dust in the lens as the skater cut through the streets. Then there were the lines. Usually, the trick took forever to land, and a painful day of *meh*-bails was his idea of a wasted afternoon. Inspiration, zero.

All gear and no idea.

He repositioned the kicker for better access to the wall beside the window. The thought was, with enough speed and scoop, he could slappy-disaster into the window-frame and wall-ride out to the floor. Whilst flipping his deck between his hands, he stood back and imagined the line. It *looked* doable. He took the run, pushed, popped, slapped the board vertically into disaster and bailed at the last second. It *was* doable. He got back into position for another attempt, then ran through the hallway, jumped on his board, and gave it one full push before arcing around on the herringbone tiles towards the kicker. Focused only on the wall edge, he didn't even feel the ollie—it was all one smooth movement—his front-foot slid high up the board, and his back leg weightlessly guided the tail to the window frame, then as soon as the board made contact he pushed on the nose and unhooked the back wheels. If anything went wrong in that instant his back truck would spit him to the floor, but it didn't. He cleared the vertical edge and felt his back wheels make momentary contact on the wall before gravity pulled him back towards the floor.

Damn, it felt good.

So good, he wanted to do it again.

He took the same line, but this time he popped much harder and earlier almost as if he was going to go for a standard frontside wall-ride, but he held his front leg high, caught the nose with his hand and smacked his tail on the vertical window frame. On the way down he realised his weight was too far forward, causing him to kick his board away and stumble across the floor. It was only a hunch he'd make it again anyway. No big deal, besides, he had a better idea: to crail-slide the window ledge. So, he repositioned the kicker, moved some more carpet out of the way, and looked back at the ledge as he walked through the hall into position to try again.

Here goes nothing.

Another run through the hall, another ollie off the ramp, catching the nose with his trailing hand, he poked out his back foot and made contact with the ledge; it slid, but he over-rotated. As he landed backwards, and with too much weight on his toes, he carved around in a semi-circle straight towards the sofa and fell into the sitting position. After he realised his good fortune at not having to fall on the filthy floor he noticed the camera's red LED light back through the serving hatch.

'Tell me you got that!' he shouted.

Dixel's head appeared through the hatch. 'Of course, I did. I got everything.'

'I thought you were still setting up the camera.'

'I was,' she said. 'For the first trick. I recorded everything else.'

Relieved at not needing to do it all again, he pushed his head back into the headrest then remembered the junkies' needles.

Oh, shit.

He then gently, oh-so-gently, got up off the sofa.

10

SLEDGEHAMMER

They quickly made their way to the middle of the building and found the main hall. It was a huge space, instantly echoing their footsteps. Pigeons twitched and cooed from the beams in the ceiling as if to discuss who had entered their home. Eight imposing windows on the south side must have been six-feet short of the entire height with only the odd broken panes of glass near the bottom. Most likely people realised the more windows they smashed the colder it would get inside and ruin a night's stay. The kitchen had been largely destroyed; appliances had been removed, or stolen, and left pipes jutting and cables dangling from the walls. Flipped tables and chairs lay scattered around except one in the middle, perfectly neat and dust free. For the guard, presumably, to sit and eat lunch.

'Spooky, yeah?' Dixel took a photo of the table with her phone.

'Don't start with all that. He's probably just bored and fed up with eating in his car every day.'

The room may have been massive but it served up nothing for skating. They soon moved on and headed for a series of smaller rooms towards the South-Western side. Playrooms for those stuck in a lost childhood; observation rooms separated with a large—now smashed—two-way mirror; a few bathrooms; more offices and a shower block. The small pane of wire-threaded, shatter-proof safety glass, gave a glimpse into each room before they entered. It was easy to imagine alarms blaring, doors locked and patients slamming fists into the windows screaming for help: to get out or get in.

'Hospital or prison?' Ethan pushed through the doorway.

They came to a laundry room with large industrial machines set in the walls like escape pods in a science fiction film. Staff garments lay scattered around the floor as if visitors had played dress-up. This room had real potential. A set of double-doors at one end of the room led to an access ramp for the laundry trollies. At the other end, a huge laundry chute dropped down from the upper level, big enough to walk into.

'Look at this.' Dixel stood at the foot of it and

peered up into the blackness. 'Do you think it opens up into the floor above?'

'Maybe, but I'd smack my head on the way up.' Ethan tapped his knuckles on the plasterboard then grabbed the edge with both hands and gave it a hard yank. It flexed, then cracked and split on one side. 'I think we've got something here.' He heaved on it again until a large section snapped away from the opening and dropped onto the floor. They had found a natural vert wall with a surface as smooth as marble. It would take some work to clear the rest of the plasterboard away, but once done it would make the perfect line from the double-doors down the trolly-ramp to the chute.

'This will be crazy. We can get this clear in ten minutes.'

'Great, but I have a better idea,' Dixel had already wandered out towards another corridor. 'You carry on whilst I'll go and see what's this way.'

'You're not helping?'

'Sort of,' she said. 'By not getting in your way.'

'Do you want the map?' He paused to hear a reply, then shouted, 'Can you at least look out for a brush?'

'Top of my list,' she shouted back.

Using his board as a sledgehammer, he swung and smashed his rear truck into the surround, wincing as splintered pieces of plasterboard narrowly missed his face. He stood outside the chute and swung in, he stood inside and swung out, and sometimes he pitched blindly up into the dark in the hope of hitting anything worthwhile. Stubborn points and larger weakened joints needed precise explosive thuds. His black Emericas turned grey to match the sleeves of his hoodie; bits of debris caught in his neckline and slid down inside. After fifteen minutes of pulling and bashing to clear all the sides and front, he now needed to clear the floor. A quick search of a nearby shower block and he'd found a brush, bucket and mop in a cupboard. The resulting dust-cloud from the brushwork caused fits of coughs and sneezes and coated his clothing further. The biggest plasterboard pieces were dumped in a laundry truck, wheeled up the ramp, and out into the cool mid-morning air. An outside tap needed two-hands to turn it before splattering cold fresh water at his feet. He rinsed his mouth out and washed his hands and face. The trees beyond the perimeter wall were now faintly visible as the fog had begun to clear. Up above, the patchy sky allowed the sunlight to fade in and out suggesting a good day was coming. Ethan took a moment to look in through the back doors and saw the line to the chute. It was a good start but it needed something extra: a Hubba.

He skated out through the Food Hall back to

the room full of cabinets and found the one with the open drawers, figuring it would be the lightest to transport back. After pulling it away from the wall and tipping it over, his board flexed and wobbled with the weight as he wheeled it gently through the doorway and back to the laundry room. Once there, he slid it off the board and dragged it into position against the wall. Though its top edge was metal, its thin construction wouldn't be able to handle an unwaxed truck without it buckling. He knew he'd only get a few hits before it eventually became un-skateable. However, it was irresistible.

After a quick sweep of the top area he set the broom against the wall and used some towels to wedge the back doors open. With a one-push run-up, he popped into a backside 50-50 to get the feel of it then jumped off his board before he hit the debris at the bottom of the chute. The truck damage on the cabinet edge was clear; it would only be good for a few go's. So he put his board to one side and got on with clearing the chute and mopping the floor as best he could. Once done, the place almost sparkled, and the urge to stay and play was tempting, but it would be a waste of energy without a camera to catch any of it.

He needed Dixel.

Corridor after corridor, room after room, door after door, each clicked open and clunked shut. Echoes rippled along with him and escaped out of the broken windows. The radiators were warm to the touch, but surely it didn't make sense to heat a whole building just for a security guard, unless there was a timer running? Ethan spotted Dixel pass two doors ahead. He thought about sneaking up and startling her, but she would have to be stone deaf for that to work. Just as he reached the final door, the power came on, and the florescent lights blinked into life. He was right, there was a timer. That would explain the heating. He pulled on the door, but it wouldn't open. It was locked.

11

THE TIMER

Dixel jiggled the door handle. Ethan tried the one behind him: it opened.

'Maybe they aren't all locked,' he said. 'I can try and find the power switch.'

'Ok. I'll see where this room leads. There's plenty of busted windows, so I'll meet you out in the courtyard if I reach a dead end.'

Ethan held up his phone to the window, 'Give me a call if you have any problems.'

She gave him a brief smile, 'Sure. Whatever.'

Ethan traced his way back through the corridors, jamming open the doors with books, chairs, and anything else he could find. Some opened, some were locked, and some would only open from one side. Even gently resting the door against the lock catch would slam it shut. Instantly, he'd push the door again to test if it opened, like a game of

Russian Roulette where the gun was a padlock and the bullet was a pain in the ass.

The power box that controlled all the doors had to be near some kind of storeroom, offices, or anywhere away from patient access. As he reached the reception area, he listened for the guard, but heard nothing and kept moving. Each office was searched, along with all wall space, and cupboards. The thought crossed his mind that the control panel could even be outside attached to a wall or in a separate building. He couldn't worry about that now; favouring the inside to be his best bet. The search continued along each hallway, the records room, the medical bays, and the dorms even though the chances of it being here were slight. Eventually, after losing count of the number of rooms he'd been in, he sat, exhausted, against the wall in a medical room. This space was empty apart from a smashed handbasin and scattered old newspapers. Against the wall, broken cable clips indicated where the phone line had been ripped out and, as he followed the skirting board across the floor, he noticed a fresh patch of white paint. A closer look revealed some words scratched into the paintwork, *Fibres are everywhere You are right 15 years They know about them LD*.

Ethan ran his fingers across the text and thought about who might have written it. Some wacko, probably spaced out on medication. At knee-level was a small white door completely sealed by years of paint. He took out his front door key, scored the paint all around the edge of the panel with it, and gently eased the tight door open. He could already sense the welcome hum of electronics, and once he illuminated the darkness with his phone light, he could see a grid of boxes, ticking and clicking within the dusty cobwebs. He'd found it.

Thank you. LD.

A fat red button in the middle of the dusty console indicated the mains trip switch: it had triggered, so there shouldn't have been any power to the building. He depressed the button and tripped it again, and again, yet the lights remained on. Someone must have fitted an electrical bypass. He followed the cabling down from the unit to the back of the wall, and found another, much newer, switch and timer. This secondary switch rendered the first obsolete. The new timer mechanism took a bit of figuring out to override the settings, but once done, the power to the floor cut off, hopefully disabling the locks. If the guard was now in the building, the sudden change would have alerted him that someone had messed with the power. Ethan shut the door and hurried through the corridors, pausing occasionally to listen for footsteps or doors shutting, in case the guard had returned. He heard nothing and kept moving.

As he passed by one of the rooms, he saw a floor fan through a gap in a door, and felt a sudden urge to return to it. He listened briefly at the door, then stepped inside. It was the guard's office. On the back of the chair was a short white jacket like he'd seen on the floor of the laundry room. On the desk, a cheap blue plastic flask with a red cup—like a child would take to school—and a carrier bag of sandwiches. A sheet of paper covered in dead bluebottles lay on the desk, each one meticulously fixed into a grid with little sticky labels. There was also a big stack of faded green files. The file for Andrew Williams contained about a dozen handwritten pages of notes, and another for Brian Wexford showed his full attendance history from arrival to leave date, spanning eleven years from 1979 to 1990. Up on the side wall, a pin-board covered in black and white portraits had handwritten notes beneath them. Some had been linked together with parcel string wrapped around different pin heads. Most of the faces matched the names on the files apart from two. Another file, placed to one side had his family name on it: Wares, C. It was the name of his mother.

The last time he saw her he was ten and she was being wheeled off in an ambulance. Despite Ethan being distraught for her to return, the social workers did a good job of keeping Heston and him entertained with distractions which peaked with a trip to Disneyland Paris, before being finally homed with a foster family. She had her issues but was never sectioned. Ubley Psychiatric Hospital was designed for long-term residents. The only long-term residency she had was with an IQ too low to look after herself, let alone two kids. Once she'd discovered alcohol and painkillers a spiral of self medicated neglect followed. He picked up her file and some sheets of paper slipped out. They weren't patient notes or attendance records like the others, but newspaper cuttings from the early nineties. Families had prosecuted the council for mistreatment of relatives; other clippings noted failed Health and Safety records; and more referred to something called Morgellons which mentioned patients claims of synthetic fibres growing from their skin.

Something made Ethan look back at the white coat on the chair. It was pressed and clean. A name badge in the front pocket read, Doctor Owens. It was the coat from the doctor he met at the hospital. *What was he doing here?* He thought. Ethan sat in the chair and studied the bluebottles stuck to the paper, then looked back over at the wall. He started to get a bad feeling about the security guard. This was some Infinite Security POOP which El Gato could clear up. He took out his phone and found his number.

. . .

When the call connected, it sounded as though a paper bag was rustling in his ear.

'Hey Edwardo, it's Ethan.'

A voice said, 'Hang on.'

Once El Gato got properly on the call he immediately started to ramble on about some staff in a QuickFit garage trying to over charge him for a new windscreen, but Ethan had no time for that and quickly cut him off.

'The guard at the old Psychiatric Hospital is one of your employees, right?'

'Ah, yes, he's a good guy, no?'

'What's his name?'

'Lewis, why?' El Gato laughed. 'Ah, he catch you, yes?'

'Lewis Owens, ok. What do you know about him?'

'I know him for few weeks now,' El Gato said. 'Great guy. I never have problems. I say, I come round, say hello, see if I can do *something*. He says, no, no, I am okay, *you* are busy, I'm fine. I tell you, I need more people like him.'

'No, I mean have you done background checks on him?' Ethan asked.

El Gato went quiet for a moment, 'Why? What is going on there? Yes, I checked him he is good. Why?'

There was a hesitancy in El Gato's voice which reminded him of his doctor saying, *This won't hurt a bit*, before jabbing a tetanus needle into his arm.

'I'm here in his office at the psychiatric hospital and there's a lot of files and reports about patients. Also, a couple of days ago when you picked me up at the hospital, a doctor spoke to me, being all weird, and I think it's the same guy.'

'What you mean, *same guy?*'

'His hospital jacket and ID is here,' Ethan paused as El Gato was distracting him. 'Look, what I need to know is: is this guy a doctor or a security guard? Because don't I think he's both. What did he do before this?'

'He, uh,' El Gato hesitated enough to make Ethan believe some bullshit was about to arrive.

'You haven't checked him out, have you?'

Ethan heard the sound of gears grinding in the van and his tone changed.

'Stay there. I am coming over.'

12

KEYS AND CODES

Ethan heard the phone click off then felt a smug glow of *gotcha* sweep over him. Feeding him some kind of bullshit like he wouldn't get found out. Now he had two problems to deal with: not only was he surer than ever Owens had a bad case of the old 'McBonkers', but Mister Super-dufus was careering across three lanes of mid-morning traffic to come to his rescue. A self-inflicted Mexican headache of epic proportions was not needed this morning. No thank you. Ethan spun himself around in the chair until his head sent a throw-up pulse to his stomach. On the desk, buried amongst a stack of papers, a sheet with a checkerboard pattern along its edge caught his eye. It was a parking warning in PCSO white, not the heavy hitter yellows from the parking-Nazis. It referenced the time and place of notice and the registration number of the vehicle, but not the name of the owner. On the back, a scribbled note: *Weds, arrival, no funny stuff.* That was it. *Weds* was today; and what *stuff* could be *funny* to warrant saying *no* to? Tickets like these were last seen scattered across the dashboard of El Gato's van. Ethan sniffed the ticket and felt his day was about to get a whole lot worse.

His phone buzzed: it was Dixel.

'Hey, where are you?' Ethan said.

'I found this cool place,' her voice echoed. 'You should come and check it out. I'll stream it.' The phone flicked to video of her fingers whilst she clipped it into a mini-tripod on the floor. When the lens focused he saw a large sweeping staircase in the middle of the room like something you'd find in a 1920s theatre. Dixel walked into shot and twirled around with her arms wide, 'Amazing huh?'

It was good to see her, she looked really happy, and in her exploratory element, but there was big fat cloud welling up in Ethan's chest.

'Get out of there,' he said. 'I think your friends from the forum might have been right about the guard.' But Dixel was too far away from the phone to hear him. She walked up the stairs and pretended to slide an invisible fingerboard down the curving handrail, then gave a thumbs-up sign towards the camera. As she walked back towards her own camera equipment, she stopped at her bag and began unpacking it. He tried warning her again. Another low-battery notification popped up on his screen. Dixel set her camera on top of her tripod, attached the battery, and dropped a tape into the drive. Ethan shouted into the phone but she still couldn't hear.

Momentarily something blocked the screen then moved away again just as quickly. As he shouted at her again to get out of there, a figure of a man appeared behind her and covered her face with a cloth. Dixel struggled, thrashing out to hit him on his head, and she wrestled with him for a good ten seconds before the scent overpowered her and left her limp in his arms. Adrenaline surged through Ethan as he helplessly watched the screen, palms sweaty, heart racing, he paced around the office, wiping his face and muttering *fuck* to himself over and over. The little screen showed the guard carrying her off out of view, until eventually their shadow disappeared too and the scene became still. He put his ear to the phone and heard some squeaky wheels of a trolley and some footsteps. The guard came back onto the screen and walked around to the front of Dixel's VX2100, studied the control panel, and then began pressing buttons randomly until the tape release mechanism opened. Ethan got a good look at his face as he walked away: it was El Gato's man, the Doctor he'd met: Owens. At that moment Ethan's screen went black; the battery was flat.

His breaths were long and slow in an attempt to calm down, whilst his heart pounded away. *Think, think*. He couldn't. His mind started to flash images of all the gruesome films he'd watched where people were kidnapped: beaten and left in a cell, strapped in a chair, unconscious and bleeding, or worse. It was easy to sit and wait, or leave and call the police or something, but all those ideas felt like running away. It would take too much time. He took the map and studied it again; he found the big room. *That must be it*. He had to assume the faded grid on the page illustrated the stairs. Then the lights in the corridors came on again: that power switch! The timer must have failed. He ran to head back towards the unit, but the door was locked. He tried to turn his phone on again, but the screen didn't even blink. All he could think about was the comments on that website, of people losing hours, calling the guard a nutter and of people being locked inside and frightened of the man. Suddenly, Ethan snapped out of his day-dream and threw the phone as hard as he could against the wall, smashing it into tiny shards of plastic and glass. He needed to get to Dixel, now. The map couldn't be trusted. She was right, N27 had fed him some bullshit again. There must be something in the office which could help him.

Within seconds he yanked the drawers out of the desk and onto the floor. A frantic search through the contents revealed nothing. Next, the cupboard: containing wet weather gear, a bee-keeper style set of overalls and boots, various stacks of files, and a small cabinet of drawers. He wrenched the unit away from its fixing, stomped on the flimsy casing until each drawer popped open, and fanned through sheets of old delivery invoices and courier paperwork. Useless. Once every obvious location had been checked, he sat in the chair and heard something metallic and heavy knock the side of the radiator. Hung on the back of the chair, inside a dark green hessian bag was the dull glint of over a hundred internal door keys on a keyring.

'Yes!' Ethan pulled them out into the light, but had no-idea which key fitted which door. The keys were all flat stamped, grubby from years of wear, and had a SGS company logo on the head. A key selected at random fitted into the lock but wouldn't turn. It was tight in the barrel without even a millimetre of play. He was sure the guard would be heading back to the office, and although ambushing him felt attractive, a pinch of fear tingled in his fingers. Too many damn corridors and not enough windows; it felt as if the air was thickening with each breath. He wiped his face, unzipped his hoodie, and flapped the pockets to create a little draft.

The locks might be good but the doors were still fifty years old and attached to the framework with screws. If everything else was crumbling to pieces the doors couldn't be that secure. The hinges probably wouldn't stand up to the hammering of a fire extinguisher slamming into it over and over. Then an idea came to him: he hadn't seen a fire extinguisher in the building yet. It's possible they might have been removed when the building was shut down, or perhaps the extinguishers were stolen much later, or never installed at all.

The corridor ceiling didn't have any signs of a sprinkler system or fire alarms but it did have smoke alarms. He grabbed a metal bin from one of the offices, found some matches in a drawer, stuffed some old newspapers inside and set the contents alight. He suddenly realised the ceiling was too high, and before the papers could burn out, he heaved a cabinet over onto its side to stand on. As the flames got going, he held the bin high above his head hoping to trigger the alarm and unlock the doors. The flames flicked out around the rim feeding off the air and blackening the ceiling. It got so hot he could barely hold it. Then something thudded into the bin.

Inside, the smoke alarm had morphed into a small lump of burning plastic pumping out a toxic black smoke. So much for the fire safety system; it couldn't even manage a beep.

It was then he noticed an A4 picture frame on the wall which must have been hidden behind the cabinet. It was an evacuation plan of the building covering three floors and inside each boxed area, a four character code in very small print. There were no room names, just codes, and they felt familiar. He'd seen them in one of the small notebooks from the desk drawers. After finding it again on the office floor he returned to the evacuation plan and saw the codes matched. Ethan flicked further on through the pages until he found the list of codes which matched with each room. He had a map he could trust at last and knew the codes but he still needed to get through all the doors.

'This is bullshit.' He punched the frame and it dropped to the floor. *Enough of the mind games*, he thought, *Let's try the direct approach*. He ran at the nearest door and pounded his heel into the lock area, again and again, and then switched sides to kick at the hinges but they didn't even wiggle. He continued kicking at the door frame until his foot hurt, then kicked it some more, until it was clear he wasn't getting anywhere. So much for fifty-years of woodworm; it was as solid as the day it was built. Ethan slumped to the floor partly to rest and partly to figure out what to do next. Dixel could be dead for all he knew. *That bastard*, he imagined thumping

Owens into unconsciousness and strapping him to a medical bed.

Then one of the keys from the bunch caught his eye. There were two characters stamped into the key head under the logo.

13

EXPERIMENTS

The two letters were HG, and on the reverse side, the number twenty-two. He found the code HG22 matched a room on the second floor.

'You're an idiot.' He laughed for not noticing earlier but the relief was short-lived: Dixel still needed to be found. The code for the door ahead: TS69. A methodical hunt through dozens of keys began by alphabetising them into piles on the floor. Now he was getting somewhere. A space on the plan past the food hall and laundry room would have been large enough for a set of stairs. It was called the Sun Room and it was the only plausible space she could have been. He traced back the shortest distance through the corridors to his location and found each key needed from the bundle. The route was twelve doors exactly.

· · ·

By the time Ethan had reached the Sun Room, it was dead quiet and still. Specs of dust floated slowly in the shafts of sunlight from the windows. The spot where Dixel's camera gear had been was empty; then he remembered her phone and found it still at the back of the room against the wall. Either Owens hadn't seen it or forgot to take it with him. Ethan switched it on, found her videos, and scrolled through several personal clips until he found the most recent. He dragged the play-head towards the end and watched the guard snatch her again. He replayed the video over a few times watching how quickly Owens clamped her head and took her weight as she went limp.

The replay hadn't helped. It was as if it had happened all over again. He shouldn't have let her go off alone. They'd both read about the rumours. He should have listened and stuck with her. He was pacing around again and hadn't realised he'd punched a hole into a partition wall. At the bottom of the media gallery were other photos she'd taken. Scrolling through them helped to calm him down. The latest shots were somewhere by on a beach with a friend. She was happy. Just seeing her smile made him smile too. It was Brighton; he recognised the pier. If there was a boat handy, he knew she'd want to jump in it and paddle out for a closer look. She'd ask him to join her, but after saying no, he also knew she wouldn't hang around hoping he'd change his mind. He found another video she'd made at Musgrave Park. A kid held the camera whilst she cruised around on that big old longboard of hers. It was good to see she was still riding but he wished she'd get a shorter one like he'd told her to.

The atmosphere in the room changed. Another person had joined him: Owens. The man looked calm and just as dishevelled as when they first met. He walked slowly around the edge of the room, shoelaces undone, trousers scuffed at the knees, a radio on his belt—he was on duty after all. The exit was too far away and probably locked. He eventually looked at Ethan and smiled one of those smiles where the eyes don't join in. Owens pulled out a chair and sat at one of the tables. He took out a sheet of paper, placed it in the middle, then took a white handkerchief from another pocket, folded it, corner to corner into a six-centimetre square and placed it in the middle of the paper. The main windows had security bars across them, and the ones which didn't were smashed and would cut a man to pieces trying to get out. After enough awkward silence had passed, Ethan needed to say something. Who knows how long this guy would take to form a coherent sentence.

'I'm guessing you're not a doctor, then?' he said.

Owens laughed a little, 'We can all have many jobs, but we can only have one purpose.'

'And what's yours?' Ethan almost wished he hadn't asked.

'Very existential,' Owens said. 'But you first. What's your purpose? Please. I'd love to know.'

Ethan searched for an answer which would possibly delay or please him. Either would do. 'I'm just skating,' he said.

'Ah. Of course.' His eyes still didn't smile. He bounced his knee under the table and shuffled his shoulders. 'But here of all places,' he continued. 'I did try to warn you. It's not somewhere you should be.'

It was as if someone had pricked the back of Ethan's neck and forced him to scratch it, 'Why not?'

'You still don't know?' he said. 'When you told me your surname, I realised your mum is Cathy, isn't she?'

The mention of his mum's name stalled his brain like a maths question. When his neurons fired up again, he said, 'What do you mean?' The answer would surely suck him into plenty of painful thoughts or potential lies but he couldn't help himself.

'She was here,' Owens said joyfully as if he was congratulating himself for his own research. 'She was ill, of course, but this is where we met. It was April and the garden had started to bloom, we talked almost every day. She was a good listener;

damaged, the others said, but I found her charming.'

Almost every day. Bullshit. Owens was either lying, trying to manipulate, or both. His mother was never here for long. She might have needed a short stay to get some space and rest but it wasn't long before she was back home again. The dust scraped his dry throat as he thought of his mother's return after her treatment. Those bottles of pills neatly lined up on the kitchen cupboard with strict instructions from his Aunt not to touch them. His mum claimed that they were poisoning her. *They* were never identified. Everyone became *They*: doctors, social workers, and anyone with an 'ology. She hated those 'ologies.

'Do you know who *they* were?' he asked. 'She always spoke of They. Do you know who she was on about?'

Owens looked delighted to fill in some obvious gaps in Ethan's knowledge, 'Here,' he announced, sweeping both hands up in the air as if planning on catching the loose ceiling tiles. 'They were all around us, for years. It's what we spoke about the most. They were infecting us all; we were all suffering at their experiments. Your mother knew that more than any of us.'

'What experiments?' he asked.

'They never said what they were doing but we all knew. They said it was just routine checks to monitor and improve our progress, but we'd been here long enough to know their procedures were anything but authorised.'

Ethan felt a breeze on his neck blow in from the smashed window beside him. 'What have you done with Dixel?'

Owens smiled. 'She's fine. I just wanted to check she was clean.' He got up out of his seat.

Just a few feet to Ethan's left was an old Castrol Oil can. If Owens came any closer he could grab it and enjoy punting it across his forehead. A scraping sound of the main gate opening distracted them both. *Dixel?* Ethan rushed to the nearest window and saw El Gato's van pull up outside the gates. *Thank god*, he thought. He couldn't remember the last time he was happy to see a security guard.

El Gato tried his key in the lock but gave up after it wouldn't open.

'I've changed the locks,' Owens said.

El Gato went back to his van and took his radio from the dashboard. The radio on Owens belt fizzed with activity and El Gato's voice said, 'Lewis, It's Edwardo.' Before El Gato could say anymore, Owens twisted the knob on the top of the radio and El Gato's voice cut off. Ethan looked back out towards El Gato and watched him fiddle with his radio, then climb back into his van and shut the door. As he reversed away from the gates, Ethan thought two things: how was he going to catch El

Gato's attention and why was there was a smell of ammonia in the air?

A cloth-covered hand clamped over his mouth. He tried to yank his head away but Owens had done this too many times before. Ethan's strength and coordination faded and he couldn't pull those fingers away from his face. Fumes squeezed his lungs in the search for oxygen. Panic set in and he lashed out with his elbows at Owen's head and ribcage, but he couldn't twist himself out of the hold. Owens followed Ethan wherever he went. A warm sensation calmed his thoughts and the panic subsided. His whole body relaxed and he couldn't struggle anymore.

This isn't so bad, he thought.

14

ZIP-TIED

The radiator pipes spoke to him in gurgles, clicks, and spits. A draft of cool air from the floor fan glanced his skin as it hummed left and right. The wheels of the chair were gunked up with dust, and the characters, H4, were crudely painted in white under the seat. Slowly the rest of the room came into focus. Ethan coughed and tried to sit but quickly gave up as something pinched and stung his wrists whenever he moved. It was difficult to tell how long he'd been there. His senses slowly began to work again. His ears were good; he smelt the mould and dust of the wooden floorboards beneath his cheek. The feeling of disorientation reminded him of a slam, but without the pain. Replaying a mental checklist would test for concussion: recalling his phone number, home address, national insurance number, debit card PIN, and finally his date of birth. With the test passed, everything seemed in place, but recalling what happened wasn't clear. It took him a while to figure out he was in the old hospital with Owens and Dixel, somewhere. That pinch again made him wince; he needed to move, sit up, and stop it hurting. In the bin, he noticed an empty packet of zip-ties. *Why couldn't it have been a rope or electrical cable?* Zip-ties were bomb-proof.

He sat and realised he was alone. He grabbed the radiator pipe and pulled it several times. It fed down through a hole in the floor which had enough space for a couple of fingers. By pulling on it again and again, up and down, he heard the squeak of nails being dragged through the woodgrain. He pulled his feet in close and pressed his back into the radiator to lift his weight off the floor. Once he'd kicked the floorboard away, he realised all that effort was wasted. The pipe fed directly beneath him into the darkness of a very sturdy two-by-four.

The struggle had given him a little more room to manoeuvre. He grabbed the base of the radiator and pulled it back and forth. The fixing must have been just as old as the flooring and the bottom fixing broke away almost immediately. It didn't take much effort to release the other side, either. Next, the top two brackets. Just as he felt he was getting somewhere, he heard Owens head back down the hall whistling as though he was delivering the post. Ethan panicked and pushed the radiator back against the wall, kicked the loose floorboard under the desk, and placed his leg over the hole.

Owens didn't even look at him when he entered the room. Instead, he turned to his desk files and the pin-board of names and faces. Mumbling, as if replaying a conversation, it felt as though he had forgotten Ethan was even in the room. He wanted to get Owens talking and find out what happened to Dixel.

'What's that for?'

Owens pulled a newspaper cutting from a file, found a free pin, and stabbed it into the board. 'Impressive, isn't it?' he said. 'This is the investigation the police should have conducted. But we are not the police. We are the guinea-pigs and this is our investigation into them.' Owens considered his board again. He seemed so proud of it, adjusting lines of string, and straightening some of the cuttings. 'Everyone here was a patient.' He pointed out a pair of connected portraits.

'How?'

'Threads.' He pinned up a Guardian article entitled, *Morgellons*. 'You know out of one-hundred and twenty-six living patients, it was the only thing that connected us all. Yet no-one spoke of it, and anyone who tried was put on a new course of medication until they couldn't remember.'

'They didn't treat you for it?'

'Oh, we were all being treated, but for what,

wasn't clear. Only when I got here I started figuring it out.'

'How long were you here?' Ethan spoke with caution in case something set him off.

'Long enough to meet your mother.' He smiled one of his fake smiles again. 'How is she doing?'

'How should I know?' Ethan said.

As if the conversation had left Owens' head, he turned back to his board and began muttering to himself again. He took a Stanley knife from the table, flicked out the blade, and used it to cut around a newspaper article. The stapler was empty, and during the hunt for more staples, he spilt the contents of a drawer all over the floor. A pair of scissors bounced under the desk and Owens hadn't noticed. He found the staples and loaded a strip into the cartridge. Ethan couldn't stop glancing at the scissors, wondering whether he could reach them and whether he could do it without Owens noticing. His wrists were sore and bloody.

'What do you want?'

'Truth!' Owens declared immediately.

'So, why am I here, like this, and why did you take Dixel?'

'Oh, it was just a routine sweep. I can't just go walking around Ubley swabbing people, can I? At least here, everyone is trespassing. They are risking their lives already. I'm doing you all a favour.'

'How?'

'If the roof collapsed on this place, I'm responsible. I wouldn't have been doing my job if I'd allowed people to roam around. And besides, the police will just laugh you out of the station.'

'You don't know that.' Ethan regretted his words as soon as he said them.

Owens smiled. A real one this time. 'You see, the real criminals are those who sanctioned and funded this place, and kept it going despite all the pleas, protests, and legal action to close it.'

His tone had changed, too. That Stanley knife emphasised his words, jabbing at news articles, and people on the board. He needed to calm down.

'What are you testing people for? Ethan asked.

'For fibres,' Owens spoke as if it was the most obvious thing in the world. 'Arms and legs mainly. Just a quick sweep of the skin, as it's clear as day if they are infected.'

'And were we?' Ethan humoured him whilst watching that Stanley knife flash around in the light.

'You're both clean,' he said with a dismissive disappointment.

Owens' radio cut in. El Gato was still trying to get hold of his employee and get into the hospital. He stepped out into the hallway and said he'd come and meet him at the gate.

Ethan seized his chance and slid as far he could along the floor. Stretching out, he managed to flick the scissors back towards him with his foot. It was awkward as hell to try to open the handles, then flip the blade round to point up into the gap between his wrists and the plastic tie. No matter how many times he tried he couldn't get the blade into position. The scissors dropped from his fingers and left him scrabbling around trying to pick them up again. After so many attempts he realised it was taking too long and needed another approach. He needed something sharper, something that could cut or burn or eat away at the plastic. The glass beaker of flies. Instinctively, he kicked the table leg and watched the little jar shuffle towards the edge. After kicking it many more times it eventually smashed onto the floor in many good-sized pieces. Once he'd got the largest piece into his hands, he rotated the shard upwards and tried to guess where the plastic edge would be. The glass shard moved slowly towards his wrist and he waited to feel something.

A clattering of footsteps slapped down the hallway outside the office as Dixel ran straight past the doorway, spotted him, and ran back into the room.

'Are you ok?'

Ethan dropped the shard of glass. 'Good timing. Help get me out of this. There's a pair of scissors behind me.'

Dixel cut the plastic band and he buried his

wrists into the loose folds of his t-shirt to hide the cuts but she'd already seen them.

'Is that from the glass?' she said.

'No, from the plastic. It was so tight.'

'I think you're going to need to get them checked out.'

'Later.' Ethan slowly got up and stretched out his stiff joints. 'What happened to you?'

'I don't know. I found myself outside on the bus stop seat.' She brushed the brick dust from her belly. 'I had to crawl my way back in again.'

'Did he speak to you? The doctor, Owens. The guard?'

'Wait, who, which one?' Her eyebrows tightened.

'It's the same guy. I saw him grab you.' He wanted to tell her everything but now wasn't the time. 'He's probably going to be back at any minute. We could hide here and jump him.'

Out of the window, Dixel saw two men by the gate. It was El Gato and Owens. 'I wouldn't be so sure of that.'

'Hermanez knows Owens is dangerous,' Ethan said relieved. 'I spoke to him earlier.'

The two men stood in the drive. Close, like friends. Ethan couldn't understand why El Gato wasn't hauling Owens off into his van.

'Whatever we're waiting for, doesn't appear to be happening. What did you tell him?'

'Everything. That Owens is a nutter and he'd taken you. I also found out El Gato employed him with no checks. El Gato said he'd deal with it.'

The two men shook hands in the car park then El Gato looked back over at the main building.

'He's letting him leave,' Dixel said. 'Are you sure you told him what he's done? Because it doesn't look like it.'

'Yes, I did,' Ethan said looking agitated. 'Maybe he didn't hear me, but I thought he did.'

Dixel had already started leaving the office. 'We've got to get out there and tell El Gato. Come on.'

15

QUITTER

They both ran out of the office, into the hallway, and through the corridors as quickly as they could towards the reception area. With just a couple of doors to go, Ethan spotted El Gato through the small window coming towards them.

'Hey,' he shouted and pushed the final door, but it stopped him dead. 'Open the damn door.'

El Gato walked up to the little window and shook his head, then leant up against the wall as if he was relaxing from a long shift with a cigarette.

'Come on, open it,' Ethan shouted again, 'Call the police. Owens is dangerous.'

Again, El Gato didn't react. He just shook his head. 'I think before I let you out we have to come to an understanding.'

'What are you talking about?' Ethan slapped the glass 'Dixel, find the key.' He thrust the little notebook into her hands. 'This door is AH34. The codes are in the back.'

'Don't bother,' El Gato said. 'The deadlock is on.'

'What do you want?' Ethan shouted at him.

'It is simple. You know Lewis is not a bad man. A little troubled maybe but your friend here is okay, so there is no harm done. He won't do it again so there is nothing to tell the police.'

'He's dangerous and you know it.'

'Look, I regard you as a friend.' El Gato slid off the wall and framed his face in the little window. 'We do not need this attention. You need to deliver your filming and I need to keep this business going. Let's not lose all we've worked for. We've all made mistakes, haven't we?'

'What do you mean by that?' Ethan said.

'You and your brother,' El Gato had a sly smile. 'I know what happened, the lady in the car, she may never wake up. But you and your brother made a plan, yes? It wouldn't be good for the newspapers to know that the local boys cheated everybody, right?'

Ethan didn't want Dixel to hear all the details, at least not without a good explanation. 'Don't change the subject. That's not what we're talking about.'

'What is he going on about?' Dixel asked. 'What happened to her?'

'Your friend not tell you?' El Gato said. 'Ok, I

Abandoned

will save that for another time. Back to business. Look, I will make you a deal, you will not mention anything that goes on here and I will not mention anything either. Besides, if you promise, you can have this back.' El Gato held up a cassette tape to the window.

Dixel pulled her camera out of her bag and checked the tape drive: it was empty. 'He's got our footage.'

It might have just been a tape but it was also his paycheque. No edit; no payment. Flint had always been consistent on that one. 'No deal,' Ethan spat.

'Are you sure?' El Gato gave the tape a little shake. 'I think you need this more than me.'

'Is that the right tape?'

Dixel packed the camera back into the bag. 'I don't know. I thought I had another, but maybe I didn't bring it.'

'Have you got it or not?'

'I don't know!' She kept searching through her bag pockets, certain another must be in the bag.'

Shit. He had to gamble. It was time to call El Gato's bluff. 'No deal. You've got the wrong tape. Dixel's got loads of tapes in her bag and that isn't the one she used today. It's empty.'

Dixel rooted around in her bag checking all the pockets.

'Show him,' Ethan said, but Dixel finally gave up her search and gently shook her head.

'You are so silly.' El Gato twisted the tape like he was wringing out a cloth. Splinters of black plastic pinged into the air. 'Oops.' He dropped the remaining pieces. 'I'm serious. No more nice guy. You need to know that we're in business, yes?'

Dixel found a backup tape still in its wrapping, but too late to fool El Gato.

'Hey!' Ethan hit the glass again, 'Unlock the door.'

'You have the codes.' El Gato walked away from the door and shouted back at them, 'I'm sure you'll find your own way out.'

Long after El Gato left, once the main door had squeaked shut, once his shadow had disappeared from the floor, Ethan stopped hitting the door and swearing into the air. 'This fucking place!'

He wanted to stay angry because he knew Dixel had questions about the accident. He could see out of the corner of his eye that she was waiting for him and, once he'd spat and swallowed his temper, she did.

'What was that about a woman?'

'Just leave it, will you?' He could tell her about the crash, about them looking after the kid, them being hailed as heroes, but sooner or later, she'd dig a little deeper. Everyone did.

'Did you kill someone?'

'Shit, no!' Ethan felt dizzy and rubbed his face to get some blood moving. He sat for a moment to

Abandoned

let the feeling pass but Dixel just saw an opportunity to rag on him further. Her mind was already spinning off like a firework. He could see it in her eyes.

'Hermanez was digging for something,' he said. 'Heston and me were in a car crash and a woman got hurt, and yes, she's in a coma, but I didn't kill anyone. It was an accident. Can you leave it?'

The conversation was awkward on the way back through the corridors. Ethan did his best to make out like he was fine but he wasn't. Heston's cheque was almost in the post and they'd been hailed as heroes for looking after the mother's kid until the ambulance arrived. If El Gato spills his guts it's going to flip their world upside-down again. The threat sat like a fat girl on his shoulders begging to be carried home. Another guard must have been in a side street that day ready to radio in the latest act of highway stupidity. Just his luck: if it wasn't CCTV, it was Security.

'I've had a shit day,' Dixel finally said breaking Ethan's train of thought. 'My mum's job is under threat from Zavier Labs right now. It could mean redundancy.'

'Fired you mean?'

'No. They're completely different. It's like manslaughter vs murder.'

'What did she do there?'

'She explored new business opportunities.'

Ethan pushed through one of the doors and held it open for Dixel. 'It sounds dull.'

'She says they want to move her sideways and her job is no longer needed, but she's contesting it. Zavier brought someone else in to oversee her work but they're just undermining her position.'

Ethan wondered why she was telling him this. 'Sorry, but I'm not really feeling like talking about your mum's job.'

Dixel put her bag on one of the trollies and wheeled across the main hall. 'We're not going home empty-handed, are we?'

She was talking about filming another piece. 'To be honest,' he said. 'I don't care. What can they do? Sack me? So, what? I'll blag a credit card and cover my bills instead.'

'Come on. You always deliver. That's what you told me.'

'I know, but stuff it. It's not like N27 have ever done me any favours. I need a holiday. I need a beach for a few weeks. What do you think? Shall we just get out of here?'

Dixel paused before opening the door. 'No,' she said. 'Your yet-to-exist credit card isn't going to cover a three-week holiday. Don't quit now because of El Gato or N27. If you have to give them footage to get paid then do that. Even if it's the worst thing ever, they're committed to paying you, as long as you deliver. They might not like it or air it but you can still get paid.' She paused and let the words sink in. 'Also, in case I haven't made you feel bad enough, do it for all the kids who are expecting a new video.'

Ethan smiled and let out a small *ffs* under his breath, 'Thanks for the guilt trip,' he said.

She was right of course, he didn't care about N27; they could shove their schedule, but he also knew the only way to kick himself out of a pissy mood was a skate. And, it was true he didn't want to disappoint those kids at the park. But he really couldn't pull himself together to bother.

'Then there's Ricard. If Flint replaces you…'

That name stung the inside of Ethan's ear and triggered a collapsed lung. 'I forgot about him.'

'That perked you up.'

'It's probably going to be shitty footage though,' he said.

'Oh, definitely.' Dixel opened the main hall door and let Ethan walk through first. 'It's really going to suck.'

They walked through another hallway and another set of doors.

'Or…,' she said.

'You're right. Let's do it.'

Dixel smiled.

16

REFILMING

To keep Dixel off the subject of El Gato's threat, Ethan explained how he saw Owens snatch her in the Sunroom. A visceral disgust made her recoil from the video clip after watching herself struggle against Owens' hold. It was like watching a horror film unfold and it frightened her to a new level. Ethan apologised for bringing it up. He felt bad for worrying her further, but she said she wanted to know. On the scale of psychopaths, Owens was far down the list. He could have done much worse. Dixel was more worried about what had happened whilst she was unconscious. It wasn't until they pushed through the final set of doors into the laundry room that they both focused on why they were still there.

Dixel dropped her bag on the floor and kicked up a plume of dust.

'Steady. I spent ages mopping this place,' Ethan reminded her.

He had done a good job of sweeping the area and cleaning out the debris from the laundry chute. He tested a little ollie on the surface and its dull thud echoed into the room above.

'You might want to move out of the way.' Ethan pushed up the access ramp towards the back doors. 'I'm going to hit that thing pretty fast and see what happens.'

Dixel moved her gear out of Ethan's path and wondered what *see what happens* meant. Once he'd wedged the back doors open with a couple of old towels, she watched him skate through the opening, down the slope, across the floor up the chute into the ceiling.

A thud sounded in the room above.

'Are you okay?'

Ethan's upside-down head poked out from the darkness. 'This is looking really good. I think I can ride into it from here.'

'Let me get set up first.' She swung her camera up to her face.

'No, not yet,' he said. 'Let's get some footage on the bank first.' His head disappeared from the gap then he re-appeared sliding down the chute on his bum. After dusting himself off, he gave Dixel a tour of his hard work.

'I've set up this filing cabinet to make it more interesting.'

Tour over.

'You don't look impressed,' he said.

'I am, but just inside.'

There was a certain way to ruin a shot, and Ethan knew if he didn't delicately steer Dixel to the best angle, she was going to get all cranky. 90% of the angles were a waste of time. He couldn't have her dicking around wasting footage being creative.

'I kind of need you to stand around here,' he said. 'Like right here.'

'So here?'

'Not really. More like where I am.'

'So by "around here" you mean "exactly here." Got it.' she said.

Then once he walked away he heard her say, 'Whatever you say, boss.'

Ethan's line started outside the building, skating in through the doors, a kickflipping down the first short slope, and setting his feet for a backside nose-grind down the filing cabinet. Before he got to the end, it jammed, and almost threw him to the floor. Dixel paused the recording and asked if he was okay.

'Yeah, of course.' He noticed the camera.

'You've got to film everything. The slams are the best bit. You need to record those.'

As much as Dixel didn't like being told how to do her job, she liked the idea of capturing a crash or slam, as he called it. Ethan's second attempt went better than the first, the kickflip was caught high and the nose-grind landed clean this time, and with time for one push before hitting the chute. He rose high up towards the ceiling, popped a little ollie, grabbed the tail momentarily and blasted back down the chute again. Dixel let out a celebratory yelp. Another thing he had to remind her of. He didn't want to have shouts and coughs and yelps from behind the camera coming out from the speakers. The only thing which stopped him from telling her there and then was the happiness on her face.

'I'm not sure I got you in the frame.' She queued up the run and watched it back on the little grainy LCD. 'See, your head went out of shot a little. Should I get further back?'

'Yeah, best to,' he said. 'You're zoomed out, right?'

'As much as I can.'

Then he noticed the flat Sony lens. 'You don't have the Death Lens on. You're going to need it here.'

She delicately wound the lens on to the body thread and felt the extra weight.

'Get close, otherwise, I'll be too small on screen.'
'Got it.'

He took another run. The same line with different tricks: a switch 180 flip through the doors, a tail-slide down the filing cabinet, and a melon-fakie on the chute. Then another run with Dixel in a different position. Ethan half-cab-flipped through the doors, backside lip-slid the hubba, and finally, backside kick-flipped the chute.

'You think you can follow me?' Ethan pointed at the doors and drew an imaginary line with his finger up to the chute. The slope was steeper than the ones he'd seen her ride at the Musgrave Park and noticed she was hesitant. 'You can do it,' he said. 'I've seen the video of you at the park. It's just the same as the mellow banks.'

'But that was in a skatepark. I had knee pads on.'

'You didn't fall off, and this is the same. Just push straight after me and you'll be fine.

Dixel still wasn't sure but walked up the slope behind him. 'You know I wasn't holding a camera then? What if you hit me?'

'I'm not going to be anywhere near you. I'll be in front the whole time.'

They both got set up outside. 'One push is all you need,' Ethan reminded her.

Dixel switched the camera on and they both rolled in through the doors with the camera held low just as Ethan instructed. She tried to keep the machine steady whilst he nollie-flipped onto the access ramp, nose slid the cabinet, and frontside-flipped on the chute. As he rushed back down it Dixel was still at the bottom—she'd hadn't moved—and there was no way to go around her. Luckily, she stepped to one side and he glanced her shoulder at full speed. They both went spinning off onto the floor, including the camera.

'You okay?' Ethan got up and rushed to check on her.

'I feel like a bus slammed into me.' She sat up and arched her back, then rubbed her stinging palms. 'The camera!'

It had skidded across the floor and rested on the other side of the room. Ethan grabbed the lens first and though it had a ding on the ring, the glass looked okay. Dixel examined the LCD which was hanging off its hinge by a few wires. Luckily the power came back on and the mechanism made it's familiar whirring noises. 'The screen is screwed,' she said. 'We can't check the footage now.'

'What about the viewfinder?' Ethan asked.

'It never worked.'

'You think the recorder mechanism still works?'

She pressed the button, heard the motor kick in, and watched the tape wheels spin through the casing window. 'I think so. It seems to be making all the right noises.'

She grabbed a roll of gaffer tape from her bag and taped up the LCD screen to the body. 'That'll hold it in place.'

'I didn't realise you'd be right there,' Ethan said. 'I couldn't stop. Let's take a breather.'

Dixel's phone rang; it was an N27 number. 'Hello,' she said.

Heston had been trying to get hold of Ethan for the last hour. Dixel told him to hang on. 'Ethan, where's your phone?'

He remembered the shattered pieces crunching underfoot as he left the guards room. 'It's out of order,' he shrugged.

'Maybe just call me from now on.' She listened to Heston for a moment then handed Ethan the phone. 'Don't throw it at anything.'

'I won't.' He cupped his hands together as if to receive a glass ornament on a silk pillow.

'We've had the edit in from Ricard,' Heston said. 'It's in the Dropbox now, you should take a look.'

'Is it worth it?' Ethan asked.

'That depends on what you call good. It's not like your edits. I thought you'd want to see what you're up against.'

Ethan promised to take a look later, then told him about the laundry chute find, the guard, and what El Gato had done. After Heston's initial reaction, he appeared to be more interested in El Gato.

'That doesn't sound like him,' Heston said. 'We've known him for years.'

'I'm telling you,' Ethan said. 'He flipped out and is now on some global domination trip. Dixel's footage was wrecked, that's why we're shooting more. No-one who wants to be out of this place more than me, right now.' He couldn't believe he was having to defend himself against El Gato.

'What the hell are you talking about?' Heston had listened for long enough and interrupted Ethan. 'You sound like the world is out to get you. You know how El Gato is. He's a bit fiery, but he hasn't lost his marbles.'

'You. Didn't. See. Him.'

'I spoke to him this morning.'

'How come?'

'It's not important. Look, everyone's okay, right? And I'm sure there's a good reason for all this.'

Heston reminded Ethan about Ricard's footage and promised to talk to him later.

The call ended.

Later? Was he going to get a good boy doggie treat or something? It looked like Dixel wanted a rundown of the conversation, but it was just another hour of his life he could do without explaining.

'Can we play a Dropbox clip on this?' he asked.

There were two 3G bars on her phone. 'It'll

need to buffer,' she said, 'but we can watch some of it.' She logged into the company account, found their Submissions folder, and started playing the latest upload. After ten seconds the clip began to stream in.

17

MOTIVATED

After a little bit of fuzzy black and white static, the grainy picture of the filmer's feet on a board rolling came into view. The camera raised to show another rider with loose trucks carving around on a pavement: it was Ricard. He hopped on and off the pavement, skipped over the drains and weaved around some pedestrians. His jacket flapped behind him like a cape. The camera was close and with no death lens, the filmer did well to keep him in the shot.

A low ledge was manualled, scooped up into a bean-plant, and hopped back onto the pavement again. The riders picked up speed on a smooth section throwing some frontside and backside power-slides. A pug on a lead got spooked and barked at the camera as it passed. The owner yanked back on the leash and swore at the skaters.

They both turned right into an underpass and for a moment the image went black until the sensors' exposure compensated. A rumble of urethane wheels echoed off the walls and they headed into the ball of light at the other end of the tunnel. A market trader unpacked some boxes, Ricard nose bumped one and carved around to a curb, slappied up onto it, and 50-50'd at speed into a curved section, before finally, hopping off and hippy jumping a bench.

The video buffered.

It was lame and Ethan knew it. The kid hadn't flipped once and there was nothing which he couldn't have done after six months of riding. To him, it was all flow and show.

'The skating is great,' Dixel said, 'but the filming wasn't anything special.'

'No. It all sucks. Bad quality everything.'

'Why? I can see it's different to how you skate but it looks fun.'

'It's just so weak.' Ethan handed the phone back. 'I don't need to see any more. It's not going to impress anyone. Kids don't want to see what they can do, they want to see what they can't. It fires them up to go out to try harder. *That* doesn't do anything. Once you've watched it, you won't need to watch it again.'

'Well, I enjoyed it.' Dixel watched the screen again as the buffer disappeared allowing the video to play some more. 'What's the trick where you wheelie?'

'Manual-roll.'

'He's really good at those.'

Ethan took another look at the screen for a few seconds then sighed.

'Ok, ok, I'll turn it off. Jeez.' She turned off the phone and put it away. 'Let's get this finished so we can get out of here. What else have you got?'

Ethan took a look at the chute. 'There's only one thing I need to do before I get out of here.' He pointed up at the hole in the ceiling, 'I want to do something into that.'

Dixel didn't look impressed.

'What?' he said.

'Nothing. I'm just waiting for instructions. God forbid that I actually add my own ideas to this project.'

The chute was good, but the hole was deadly. All that bashed out plasterboard and wood looked as smooth as a whistle when he cleared it, but now, up close, it wasn't looking so polished. It looked damn evil, like jumping into the jaws of a monster.

'I want to nose-pick on that ledge just inside the lip.' He pointed up into the ceiling. She shone her phone torch up into the darkness and struggled to see what he meant.

'There,' Ethan pointed. When she still couldn't see it he ran up the transition to almost touch it, before she realised.

'That's not a ledge,' she said. 'That's a piece of plastic.'

Besides, she thought a nose-pick sounded gross until he demonstrated on the filing cabinet what it looked like.

'I think you should stand right at the base of the chute.' Ethan positioned himself where he wanted her to be and pretended to hold a camera. 'You can get me coming towards it and then pan across all the way up.'

'No chance. You hit me last time!' Dixel held the camera up to her face and then remembered the viewfinder didn't work.

'You'll have to. I'll be a speck on the screen otherwise.'

'I'm not paid enough to do this,' Dixel grumbled whilst moving into position.

Once Ethan was back at the start of his line, he shouted, 'Let me know when you're recording.'

'Hit me again and I'll batter you with the camera.'

'What's that?'

'Nothing. Ok, go.'

Within a few seconds, he flew in through the opening, down the hubba, across the floor, rushed past Dixel, and straight up the chute into the darkness. All faster than she could comprehend. He grabbed frontside and planted his front truck on the small lip, then as the gravity pulled him off, he fell past much of the vertical section, landed on the transition and whizzed past her again.

'Yeah!' she shouted. 'That looked great.'

Ethan came back and stopped just before her. 'First attempt, as well.'

The problem was it felt a bit quick and simple. He expected it to take a couple of tries but to get the first one, that created a problem: it didn't look hard enough.

'Shame we can't re-watch it,' Dixel pressed down a loose piece of gaffer tape around the LCD.

'Are you sure you got it?'

'I think so, I did exactly what you said.'

He looked back up at the ceiling hole again. 'I think we should grab another angle. Just in case.'

'Thanks. Like I've never pressed a record button before.'

'I believe you, but I'm just saying having another angle will give you something extra to edit together.'

Making the move look harder than it already was, meant either dropping the Death lens or changing the angle to show the height.

'Let's try it from above.'

. . .

They made their way to the upper level and found the room directly above the laundry room. At the back, near the wall, the hole in the floor glowed from the light below.

Dixel knelt for a closer look. 'Wow. It looks so high up from here.'

The damage from ripping apart the chute left sharp edges like saw teeth ready to draw his blood. Ethan tucked in his t-shirt. The hole looked smaller than from below and the transition looked tiny. The little ledge he nose-picked on had been nothing more than a plastic case containing wires for the wall socket—its flimsy build flexed as he tested it with his foot.

'It looks fine to me,' he said wiping his palms on the back of his trousers. 'It's an optical illusion.'

'Really?' she picked at one of the nails jutting out of the lip. 'Rather you than me.' Her nervous laugh didn't make him feel any better. 'Are you sure you want to do this again?'

'Of course.' He spun his board around in his hands. Ricard would never be able to do anything like this. 'You stand here,' he directed with his hands up to his head as if holding the camera, 'and just point it down. You should be in the right position.'

Dixel took up the spot. 'Like this?'

Ethan held up his thumb. 'Perfect. I'll shout when I'm about to go.'

. . .

During the walk back down he almost decided against it. He was sure Dixel would have caught the first attempt, even without the viewfinder to watch the replay. How bad could it be? It's hard not to get the shot with Death lens. The bigger worry was if Ricard's footage impressed Dixel, it may impress Flint too. There was no way that he was going to risk Ricard getting his foot in the door any more than he already had. He tried to not think about the damn hole in the ceiling anymore. It was either going to work again or it wasn't.

Ethan stepped out through the back doors, wiped his face, and pulled on his t-shirt a few times to cool himself down. 'Ok, here I go,' he shouted.

18

CAMERA AXON

Ethan powered down the slope faster than ever and shuffled his feet into position. The only thing he focused on was the tiny plastic cable cover as he rode up into the darkness of the chute.

That was the last thing he remembered.

Everything went black.

Thoughts zipped through his mind like the view from a train window. His eyes rattled left and right inside his lids trying to grasp at something stationary. The noise between his ears rang like a finger circling a wine glass. The wind had been knocked out of him but nothing hurt: that pain would come later. He eventually, rolled over onto his side, body numb, groggy, and with no sense of balance to sit up or speak. Whenever he tried to move or open his eyes —neither worked. It felt like his brain was still ricocheting off his skull. Dixel sat close with her hand on his side talking, but he couldn't understand a word. As his senses settled, his adrenaline dissipated, his endorphins and dopamine too, his capillaries opened which allowed for more blood flow and with it, more pain. His shoulder hurt first, then his hip, then his neck, while the dull thud on the side of his head comforted him like the warmth of a pillow.

'Are you okay?'

He heard Dixel say. He groaned back.

'Should I call an ambulance?'

The thought of a medic arriving alarmed him enough to mumble, 'No,' then, 'I'm okay,' a moment later, despite not actually knowing if that was true. He couldn't yet feel his lower limbs or move one of his arms due to that shoulder.

The coordination needed to get up still wouldn't happen. *Getting up*, required a lot more concentration than usual. *Up*, and all it's complexities needed to be negotiated because he still didn't have an *up*, or a *down*, or an awareness of balance. Balance was definitely in a traffic jam, stuck behind all the pain. And there was a lot of it. Once all the versions of Dixel came into focus, he realised she was still asking if he was okay. The dumb bit of his brain knew without hesitation that he was fine, however, the smarter bit stuttered like a flip-book animation. His hip throbbed. Lots of little bones in his neck crunched as he turned his head from left to right.

Abandoned

He couldn't recall if it was always like that and yet that damned shoulder still hurt the most. It appeared that one shoulder didn't match up with the other. One was significantly lower, a whole five centimetres lower.

'I think it's dislocated.'

The pain in his voice only worried Dixel further, 'I'm calling an ambulance.' She pulled out her phone.

'No,' he insisted. 'We can just pop it back in.'

'We?' She pulled the phone away from her ear. 'I don't know how to do that.'

'It's easy.' With his weight on the other arm, he managed to sit. 'Just take hold of my hand and pull it out sideways and it'll pop right back in.'

'I could trap a nerve or something'

'So could a medic,' Ethan stressed. 'Except it'll take an ambulance crew ten minutes to get here and three hours in the hospital which I could do without if you just pop it back in. Let's just try this, please? I promise I won't sue you.'

Dixel took hold of his limp hand and wrist and with one short, sharp and painful yank to the side the arm clunked back into its socket. He grabbed his shoulder, screamed in pain, and rolled over clutching it.

'Oh shit, sorry.' She apologised, again and again, asking if he was okay.

Within seconds Ethan knew it had worked. The sharp pain switched for a dull throbbing ache.

'It's okay,' he said. 'You've done it; it's feeling better already.'

Dixel put her hands to her face like on a horror poster, 'Are you sure?'

The feeling in his fingers started to return and the movement in his arm too. He stood and paced around, cupping his hip and walking off the rest of the pain. 'I think I've had enough of this place.'

Dixel realised that they should have quit whilst they were ahead but resisted the urge to remind him of it. In between Ethan's heavy breaths and subsiding groans of pain, she noticed the cooler cloudy wind fluttered leaves against the windows. Without the sunlight, the building felt colder and any trace of excitement the Hospital previously held was gone.

As Dixel packed up her things Ethan wanted to know what happened exactly but she couldn't explain it. Saying, *You just fell*, wasn't helpful. Neither was, *Went down*, and *Hit hard*.

'You think we've got enough footage to make an edit?' he asked.

'Plenty.' She wrapped her camera in a t-shirt. 'I've got loads of b-roll footage too. That tape El Gato wrecked wasn't the only one I filmed with. I forgot I put the other tape in my jacket pocket.'

El Gato, Ethan remembered. 'What should I do about him?'

Dixel stopped what she was doing, as if waiting for a reaction or exploring a thought, then said, 'I know some people who could bundle him in the back of a car, drive him somewhere remote, and leave him there.'

'Really?' Ethan was surprised but the more he thought about it…

'No, of course not. You idiot. And what the hell do you mean, *What should I do about him?* Nothing of course. Just stay out of his way.'

Ethan pushed the thought of seeing El Gato buried up to his neck in sand from his mind and sighed to himself. 'It sounds like I'm not going to be able to ignore him. I told you, he's making it his business—literally—to get in my way and everyone I know.'

'You know other people?' Dixel joked with a smile.

'Ha-ha.' Ethan didn't smile back.

'Chill, Mr Sensitive.' She put her rucksack on her back and picked up her board. 'Let's go. I've still got work to do tonight if Flint needs this by the morning.'

They walked back through the corridors and each time she pushed through the doors Ethan heard the familiar sssssshhuunk-click sound as they closed behind him. He couldn't stop thinking about how the last edit was swapped out for her own. The more he thought about it, the more he couldn't hold back from asking.

'You're going to submit my footage this time, right?'

She banged her shoulder on one of the doors. 'What did you say?'

Ethan held the door open. 'Nothing.'

19

JUNK FOOD KNIVES

That night the temperature dropped. When the sun rose through the buildings the following morning it cut dried shapes in the road and left the shadows with a metallic sheen. Commuters weaved around the pavement, frustrated at their screen time being interrupted. Coughs hung in the air from the Metro man who handed out papers with holiday bright teeth.

N27's receptionist of ten years had been replaced by a mid-forties man with a side-parted haircut and wire-framed glasses. His smile encouraged conversation but quickly switched to duty once he realised Ethan wasn't walking towards the desk.

'It's fine.' Ethan held up his ID. 'I'm a local.'

The receptionist stepped out from behind the desk, trying to focus a little harder on the flashed ID which disappeared quickly into his pocket. The gentleman let a muscle twitch from the corner of his mouth, as Ethan reached the stairs and began his long slow walk to the tenth floor.

Through the window of the forth—when his legs started to feel shaky—he saw the 11a bus arrive. On the fifth, he saw Dixel cut across the car park drinking from her water bottle. By the sixth, Heston's car was visible parked alone in an entire row of disability bays. Floors seven to eight dragged until a couple of people entered the stairwell a floor below and forced him to focus on his steps. As they got closer he tried to straighten up and look like walking wasn't a problem, but who was he kidding? Just at the point where he rounded the stairs to the ninth floor, they exited the doors.

For a moment he paused and wiped his face with his sleeve, then pressed on.

Once out into the lobby of the tenth he sat on one of the chairs and let the moment pass. It was ten past ten and he was late. A conversation in the office behind him caught his ear: it was Heston's voice. He usually worked on the third floor, so he must have been caught with an important call on the way to their meeting with Flint. The conversation was a quiet one—and there's nothing more attention-seeking than a whisper—yet Ethan gave up trying to eavesdrop until he heard Hermanez' name mentioned. Everything else was garbled or hushed and it wasn't worth the ear-strain. He'd ask Heston another time what it was about.

'Hey you,' Dixel shouted as she came out of the elevator. 'We're late. Come on.' She screwed the lid back on her water bottle.

'Heavy night?'

'Oh, this? No. I hydrate.'

'You're on a health kick?'

She slowed her *No* down as if it was being peeled off a smooth surface.

When he got out of his seat Heston slapped him on the shoulder and told him to get a move on.

'The results are in, slacker.' Heston held up a wad of printouts. 'Do you want to know who won?'

'There was a contest?' Ethan asked. 'Don't tell me, Ricard? People liked it?'

'I'm not going to lie to you.' Heston tucked the papers under his armpit and slotted his hand into the crutch. 'They did.'

'By how much?'

Heston glossed over the detail and said he didn't have time to inspect the number fully yet. 'It was by enough.'

'Really?' Ethan looked at Dixel for some kind of justification.

'What? I completed the edit last night, uploaded the file, and crashed. I was dead to the world until an hour ago. Have you watched it?'

'I didn't have any WiFi last night or this morning.' Ethan glanced at Heston.

'Sofa surfing again?' Heston said.

Ethan didn't need to reply

'Are you homeless?' Dixel asked.

'No. I've got options. I just don't like them.'

'There's a spare room at my house if you're desperate.'

'Once he's in you'll never get rid of him.' Heston smiled at her.

Ethan took the dig but didn't retaliate. 'So, anyway, did the edit come together okay?'

'Yeah, great,' Dixel swept her hair back off her neck. She handed him a little USB stick. 'This is for you.'

'I don't need a copy, thanks.'

'It's your slam. I thought you might want to see it.'

Bonus. He took the stick and thanked her.

As they reached the office, Flint and Ricard could be seen talking through the window. Ethan held the door open for Heston, and as Dixel passed him she quietly mouthed, 'You killed it.'

Exactly forty-seven minutes later, Flint stepped briskly out with a smug smile. Ricard was the first to congratulate Ethan on his edit.

'The spot was mad,' he told Dixel. 'It'll be a cult

classic.' Which was a polite way of acknowledging the figures weren't high enough to score Flint-points.

Ethan stared at the sheet of viewing figures before pushing them back across the table for Heston to collect. 'I guess I couldn't sustain those numbers forever.'

'Stats are like that though,' Ricard said. 'Sometimes they're good and sometimes the sun comes out and they're down. I am blown away, though,' Ricard said. 'The shares were mental and by so many people I don't even know. If it wasn't for them, it wouldn't have got, what was it? twenty-six?'

'Nearer twenty-seven thousand,' Heston confirmed. 'And you can expect that to double by the end of the day.'

Ricard placed his hands behind his head and blew out a lungful of disbelief. Ethan stood and shook his hand. 'Nice one. I've got to run.'

Ethan went to the bathroom, punched the mirror. Once he'd realised what he'd done, he ran his bloody knuckles under the cold tap. He couldn't get Ricard's footage out of his head. Seeing him cruise around, ollieing nothing more than a few inches most of the time, up and down curbs. The most entertaining part of the edit was when Ricard confronted a shop owner who complained about a little wall ride on his shutter. The exchange was funny, Ethan had to admit, though he stifled his laugh when everyone else was crying. Ricard got down on his hands and knees and inspected the damage then mocked the owner begging him not to call the police. Then he went into the shop and bought three baskets of junk food to win over the owner. In the end, the owner stood in the doorway waving him off and telling him to come again. It wasn't skating, it was a gimmick, and shouldn't have been aired.

Ethan dried his hand as best he could with the hand towels and wrapped his knuckles in toilet paper. It was the first thing Dixel noticed when he returned to the hallway, but he just brushed it off as nothing and an accidental knock.

It wasn't until they were both in reception again that Dixel decided to ask how he was feeling, 'You're not pissed at Ricard are you?'

After a thoughtful silence, Ethan said he wasn't. 'Flint said times are changing. Skateboarding isn't changing: it's the same as it ever was. I mean, you saw his footage. It was all over the place.'

'True.' Dixel realised it was almost the complete opposite of the edit she had produced. 'It was just different. Don't worry about it.'

'Oh, I'm not worried.'

'You sure look like you are. Heston told me that people weren't even talking about N27 before you started these shows, so Ricard had a leg up from you. Besides, people are bound to be all over something new. That doesn't mean they'll keep watching.'

What niggled Ethan the most was not that Ricard's numbers could be incorrect but that Flint could be right. She couldn't have come to that conclusion by herself. Ricard must have told her. Even if it looked like skateboarding was changing; it never really does. Fads might come and go but solid tricks never died.

'It doesn't make me feel any better either,' Dixel said. 'I mean, perhaps I could have filmed it better or cut it another way?'

'Who knows,' he said. 'Maybe, but it probably wouldn't have made much difference. Your filming was good. I know you like it, but that location sucked from the start.'

'Let's not make that mistake next time,' Dixel said. 'Why don't we start now? We know it's coming up, so let's think of something which'll blow people away. Have you got any ideas?'

Ethan walked out through the reception doors, turned, and looked up at the building. 'Have you ever been on the roof?'

'I'm not filming anything on the roof.'

BOOK 3: POOL STAKER SAMPLE

1
THE FOUNTAIN OF DEATH

If you wanted to find zombies, simply head for the library. Those who began as fresh, imaginative, playful children would, over time, become a subdued white noise of dull adults. Life drained of blood, slow-moving soulless corpses.

The doom-factory didn't start out that way. Designed by Spanish architect, Maria De Soto Mayor, this blood-red building poked out of the tombstone grey horizon of shabby retail premises and thrust its goth-black A-frame spires into the clouds, as if Death itself needed a boundary fence. Its walls met the ground with tiny transitions which flowed into an organic brick pump-track as if it had tree roots spanning out in search of food. It pulled in anything with a pulse towards its tiny, boring mouth with a ray of stupid sunshine.

The only people it couldn't devour were the

skaters. The inside never appealed when the outside was so incredible.

In the centre of the fountain was a pair of mosaic breasts coming out of the ground.

When the Journal caught up with De Soto Mayor, she was scrubbing the graffiti off and explained the breasts, 'Represented family and community.' She then said *screw you* by posing for a photo between two jets of water from its nipples.

Ethan ollied up over the fountain wall, landed on the B-side transition, and pumped across the multi-coloured surface. The Spawn album clipped the limits of his headphones, replacing the sound of children laughing, chirping birds, and leaves in the wind.

The fountain was only available to ride once a year when it was drained for cleaning. Today it buzzed with kids on their boards, trying to slash up to the lip and stick a grind worth sharing online. A few kids noticed Ethan and moved to the sides to watch. He hated that, but knew, like them, he had to seize the chance to ride.

During previous years, each attempt to ride resulted in a voodoo powered slam, collision, or near-death experience. He'd rather not be watched as the kids always expected to see him do something amazing—which was one of the downsides to having thousands of subscribers on Network 27's video channel. And as much as he hated being sponsored by N27, he just couldn't walk away from that paycheque, just yet.

When he started at the company, the biggest perk was the private health cover. His issues were the first appointment booked in praying for the hope for a *condition*.

'It's my ears,' he told the doctor.

He didn't have a clue what he was asking for, but the medicals were five-star rated, so why suffer. The doctor asked all the pre-test questions whilst stabbing a biro in the relevant check-boxes. In a dance around the obvious, Ethan decided not to mention it affected his riding: that would get him sacked, and; he also couldn't say the Fountain scared the life out of him: that was just weak. Instead, he chose to lead the doctor down a blind alley of complaints and hope for a suitable, albeit unlikely, diagnosis. A sympathy card would have been a blessing, a free pass, an excuse: *Shit, mate. I would, but I've got this ear-thing.*

No chance.

The kids watched as Ethan carved up to the lip and felt a clickity-click under his back truck. The pump down and back up again begged for something different. On any other transition his back truck would have dropped into a smith, but with nothing to lock into he slipped his wheels over into a lip-slide, held the slide until it almost stopped, then rocked the board back in again.

In the back of his mind, he couldn't shake off the slams of previous years. The Fountain had had a bite and knew Ethan's blood tasted great. Still, he couldn't resist squeezing his fat body of hope through a small window of opportunity.

Once again, he carved across the tiles to the opposite side of the Fountain. He could have tried a crook-grind, a tail-slide, or even a lip-slide, but no, he was determined to keep it simple.

It didn't matter.

Fate played its card anyway.

Just as he committed to a rock and roll slide, a kid in a bright yellow t-shirt rolled into his peripheral vision. Ethan held the slide for three seconds at full speed. His feet were good, the wall slid well, his weight was spot-on, but that kid was there, glowing like a ripe zit. Was the kid riding towards him? He couldn't tell. Was he stepping off his board or falling off?

It didn't matter. His concentration was lost.

On the way in from the rock, his front wheel caught on the lip which shifted his foot across the grip tape and landed heel heavy. As soon as his weight settled, his board shot to the right and slammed him into the floor. His shoulder took the hit, then his head, ribs, and hip.

A wheezy grunt of lung-dust stifled every swear word in his vocabulary as Marilyn Manson sang *Trip Like I Do* into his ears.

Abandoned

He was getting tired of this. Riding never used to be this random. Sometimes after a slam—even if it wasn't too bad—the floor felt safe and soft like a bed of embarrassment whilst his skin burnt with regret and hopeful sympathy. Welcome to the Fountain, again. *Damn water features*. Ethan rolled onto his back and saw a silhouette step into the light.

'You alright?' The voice was familiar.

'Yeah.' Ethan lifted his hand to his eyes. It was his mate, Ren.

'Shame.' Ren walked off again.

Ren hadn't been seen for months and though Ethan knew he'd run into him some time, he was beginning to believe he'd been ostracised completely.

'Hey, wait up.' Ethan rolled onto his side. 'I think I broke a rib.'

Ren looked back. 'You just slapped some fat.'

OTHER TITLES

Read the rest of the Ethan Wares Skateboard series now:

Book 1: The Blocks
Book 3: Pool Staker
Book 4: Punch Drunk
Book 5: Nutbar DIY

AUTHOR'S NOTE

If you liked this story and would be interested in reading more, you can join my mailing list at https://skatefiction.co.uk and become one of my beta readers who get early access to new stories, give feedback, and receive reader copies in advance.

If you loved the book, please leave a positive review wherever you purchased it as this is the main way good books spread and help people discover me.

Thanks - Mark

ABOUT THE AUTHOR

Mark Mapstone is a UK skateboarder, writer, and author of the Ethan Wares Skateboard Series books.

After discovering there were no fiction books written for skateboarders with realistic skateboarding in them, and being qualified with a degree in creative writing from the prestigious Bath Spa University, Mark decided he was perfectly positioned to cater this audience.

In-between road-trips, an infinite Instagram feed of videos to watch, and discovering bruises on himself which he has no-idea how they got there, Mark uses his knowledge of the current skateboarding world to create exciting and authentic stories which every skateboarder goes through daily.

Follow Mark on Instagram: @7plywood.

© 2021 Mark Mapstone

Published by Credible Ink Publishing

Forth edition

No part of this publication may be reproduced, stored or transmitted in any form or by any means, electronic, mechanical, photocopying, recording, scanning, or otherwise without written permission from the publisher. It is illegal to copy this book, post it to a website, or distribute it by any other means without permission. This novel is entirely a work of fiction. The names, characters and incidents portrayed in it are the work of the author's imagination. Any resemblance to actual persons, living or dead, events or localities is entirely coincidental. Mark Mapstone asserts the moral right to be identified as the author of this work.

All rights reserved.

Printed in Great Britain
by Amazon